Editor **Dalit Nemirovsky**
Producer **Dafna Barnea**
Producer & Adviser **Mati Broudo**
Researcher/Writer **Anat Rosenberg**
Introduction **Gal Uchovsky**
Photography **Natan Dvir**
Graphic Design **BigEyes Agency, Lahav Halevy, Shachar Cotani**
Printed in Tel Aviv by **A.R. Print House**

Although every effort has been made to ensure that the information in this book is as up to date and as accurate as possible at press time some details are liable to change.

Israeli library cataloguing in publication data.
A catalogue record of this book is available from the Israel Library.

ISBN 978-965-7521-00-7

Additional Photography
p. 40 - middle photo courtesy of Benedict; p. 41 - middle right photo courtesy of Benedict; P. 50 - photos courtesy of Levontin 7; p. 51 - photos courtesy of Rugine; p. 52 - top photo courtesy of Roni Kantor; p. 70 - both bottom photos courtesy of Atlas Hotels; p. 77 - bottom middle photo courtesy of Arbitman's; p. 112 - top photo courtesy of Ronimotti; P. 115 - bottom right photo courtesy of Atlas Hotels; p. 137 - bottom right photo courtesy of Samy D.; p. 174–175 - photos courtesy of Elemento; p. 176 - bottom photos courtesy of Aisha Gallery; p. 180 - top section photos courtesy of Poyke.

Cover photo **The Orchestra Square (Habima Complex)**

Contact
Crossfields TLV
POB 14029, Tel Aviv 61140, Israel
info@cftlv.com
www.cityguidetelaviv.com

# CityGuide**Tel Aviv**

# CONTENTS

Dear Readers,

I am delighted to introduce the third edition of *City Guide Tel Aviv*.

They say the third time's a charm, and it really is. In the three years that have passed since our second edition, Tel Aviv has become even more exciting than before and has grown into a more tempting destination for visitors.

With this edition, we aim to bring to our readers and Tel Aviv's visitors a more extensive overview of the city's offerings, and to present Tel Aviv to you as it is in our eyes: a dynamic, hedonistic, multicultural Mediterranean metropolis that can easily compete with any major European city in terms of culture, fashion, culinary offerings, nightlife and leisure activities.

Our goal in creating this guide is to present this unique and interesting Levantine metropolis to visitors from all over the globe. Between these covers, we have put together the best places to eat, drink, shop, sleep and explore the city in order for visitors to enjoy Tel Aviv the way we enjoy it.

All the texts, photography and design were commissioned especially for this new edition in order to keep the book as updated and fresh as possible.

We have divided Tel Aviv into five distinct areas—the heart of the city, the center, the north, the south and Jaffa. Each chapter begins with an introduction that covers the area's history, characteristics and major landmarks. Following the introduction, you will find detailed listings and descriptions of the area's most notable dining, entertainment, nightlife, shopping, hotels and cultural offerings.

I hope this book will guide you well within this unique city that, above all, is a city that gives you the feeling you have arrived at home.

I will use the words of Gal Uchovsky, who wrote the introduction in the following pages and advises you to let yourselves feel the special flow pulsing through this city. Go with the flow—it won't disappoint you.

Enjoy,

**Dalit Nemirovsky,**
**Editor**

## THE ART OF BEING A TEL AVIVIAN

**Gal Uchovsky**

The second time is always better. The first time, you worry a bit: Maybe you won't explain correctly what it is you want to say. Maybe no one will want to listen. Maybe you're just wrong, or misleading. But the second edition of *City Guide Tel Aviv* (and the first for which I wrote an introduction) was a great success both in English and French, and my modest foreword also garnered some positive feedback. In my most glamorous moment, my idol, Morrissey (for those living on another planet, formerly the lead singer of the Smiths), who visited Tel Aviv, told me that my closing sentences were wonderful. What could be more exciting than a compliment from one's favorite poet? But we'll get to that later…

The second time is also more challenging. In the three years that have passed, Tel Aviv and the world took an additional step closer to one another. Mentions of the city in more than a few prestigious travel magazines and Web sites as a "hot spot" continue to do their part. Those who arrive here now know more about Tel Aviv than the pioneers who got here before them. Not coincidentally, new guests (you're not tourists—tourists don't read our book; tourists don't interest us, we prefer guests) have more hotels to choose from, more noteworthy places to visit, more information at their fingertips about what Tel Aviv has to offer. Our city has developed a great deal in recent years. Our mayor adores projects and complexes, and hasn't for a minute stopped working and constructing. Since the first edition of this book was published, the beachfront promenade has been extended to reach Bat Yam in the south and Herzliya in the north, and it now measures more than 20 kilometers in length. If you're into jogging or even walking, there's nowhere more fun for that than our *Tayelet*. In the north, the old port also has developed, while in the south there's an amazing new park, Midron Jaffa. Not far from there is Hatachana, which was erected on the ruins of the old station for the Jaffa-Jerusalem train line. But complexes are kind of tourist traps—you always have to be suspicious of them and make sure you don't get there on a Saturday or holiday, when they are overrun with parents from all over the country and their rowdy children. Although it might be nice, as a guest, to see our entire nation having fun. It's not easy, but it's certainly an experience.

Ibn Gvirol Street has undergone a renovation and is now more pedestrian-friendly and amenable to bike riders. Rabin Square, next to City Hall, also has gotten a nice facelift. Even Rothschild Boulevard got an upgrade, and now faces an exceptional plaza designed by artist Dani Karavan between Habima Theatre and the Mann Auditorium. All along the boulevard there are now more successful restaurants and cafés than ever before, and Rothschild appears to be the beating heart of this city. But keep in mind, as we've already explained, in Tel Aviv the issue isn't the specific place you arrive at; the issue is the groove, the mood, the ability to assimilate without anyone suspecting that this is your first visit.

Every morning in Tel Aviv is an opportunity to drink superb coffee at one of our popular cafés. (In fact, one of the things real Tel Avivians have been most proud of in recent years is our ability to prevent Starbucks from gaining a foothold here.) Then you can go for a lazy stroll that starts in the late morning or early afternoon and ends just before evening. That's assuming you haven't arrived here in August, the time of year when it's best to take cover in an air-conditioned room from 11 a.m. until about 5 p.m. Our beachfront is active from March until about December, and if you make it to the right beaches, you can enjoy a perfectly mixed margarita, after which you'll be much friendlier.

Tel Aviv isn't a city of attractions. For that, there's Jerusalem—home of the Western Wall, Dome of the Rock, Yad Vashem. You'll get there. In other words, there's nothing in Tel Aviv that you can't miss, and if there is such a thing, there's no chance you'll miss it. Tel Aviv is small, accessible and friendly. All of Tel Aviv's secrets will reveal themselves to you relatively easily, if you know how to search for them—and even if you don't. Tel Aviv isn't shy and it doesn't hide. It's a city that loves to scream, make noise and expose everything—and, if possible, it prefers to do so inexpensively. To prove my theory, one of the city's trendiest places right now is a restaurant that serves up really simple food that is, well, cheap. Chef Eyal Shani's Miznon ("Cafeteria") isn't just the most popular and extreme example of this—it's a way to understand the psychology of Tel Aviv. Shani is one of the most famous chefs in Israel: His participation in the local reality show *Master Chef* crowned him as the "poet of tomatoes" because of his tendency to refer to them using terms normally saved for fair maidens. Shani has other restaurants that are more expensive and stylish, but he recently opened Miznon, where he sells small, inexpensive dishes out of a space that was once a shawarma stand. Of course, some Tel Avivians complain that the inexpensive dishes are too simple, but locals here always like to complain about something. In any case, you should take into account that there'll likely be a line here—and it'll provide an opportunity for you to experience how much Israelis dislike lines, and how they masterfully figure out ways to circumvent them. Don't take it too hard, and take it for what it is: an experience.

Here's another tip, this time for meeting someone in Tel Aviv. There's a good chance that anyone you meet here will be nicer and have more spare time than your busy acquaintance in New York. But, in reality, who doesn't already know someone from Tel Aviv? If, by chance, you haven't met any Tel Avivians before your visit, you'll quickly make friends here. Everyone at the reception desk at your hotel will know how to point you toward the right restaurant; every waiter at the restaurant will be able to point you in the direction of the right bar or party or hangout. We truly believe that we all know everything in Tel Aviv. Within two days here, you'll be able to figure out your way to any destination by yourself.

If we return to geography for a minute, the real Tel Aviv extends from the Yarkon River in the north to Jaffa in the south—all in all, a small patch of land, but one that is lively and full of special effects. For the Church of the Nativity, you'll have to travel to Bethlehem, but the good news is that it's only an hour and a half from Tel Aviv and you can always make it back by the evening. And if it's antiquities you're looking for, there are plenty in Jaffa. If you truly want to feel like a tourist, you can climb up to the sleek restaurant wrapped in plate-glass windows on the top floor of the Azrieli Center, where on a clear day you can see Israel almost in its entirety: from Ashkelon to Haifa, and as far east as the Jerusalem hills. For conservatives among you who prefer a preliminary introduction to get a feel for a place, there is also a line of red convertible tour buses that will be glad to show you around the city.

So welcome to Tel Aviv, the city of falafel and sushi. The former should be consumed standing up, while remembering that there's always a hole in the pita from which tehina will dribble onto your shirt; the latter will be served to you at a restaurant that might be overpriced, particularly in relation to the quality of the Mediterranean fish that the proprietors use. But in order to make things simpler, getting dressed to go out in Tel Aviv is easier than in any city in the world. Even Trinny and Susannah, who made their way here this year from London, understood that the magic word here is "casual." A cotton T-shirt is the most essential piece of clothing here, and if yours happens to have an interesting graphic printed on it, you might even be rewarded with some compliments from passersby. If you forgot to pack this "it" item, Tel Aviv is the T-shirt capital of the world, and our guide includes all of the shops where you can find the most creative styles. No one comes to Tel Aviv to discover what the Lanvin collection for next season is going to look like, but quality cotton can always be found here. Still, if you wait long enough at Cantina or Brasserie, Alber Elbaz will probably show up at some point. The adored designer for Lanvin is one of the Israelis we are proudest of, and he visits us once or twice a year.

That's it. Now we've really reached the end. I wanted to write something new for my conclusion, maybe suggest a good iPhone application for you to use—but they are kind of unnecessary in our small city. Not to mention that Morrissey thought quite highly of my original conclusion, and since he's the man who wrote some of the most beautiful texts in rock history, I'll allow myself to conclude exactly as I did the last time. Here you go:

So what is the ultimate Tel Aviv experience? What is the one thing you must do, otherwise your visit will have been pointless? There is no right answer to that question. Perhaps because there is no such thing as the one, ultimate Tel Aviv experience. Tel

Aviv is a city that goes with the flow. Each morning it decides anew what is interesting, what is annoying and where we are going. Perhaps the only way to conquer the city is simply to come over—to settle in and let it pull you into its gentle flow. Something will definitely happen. Something always happens in Tel Aviv. And with a little luck, it will happen to you.

**Gal Uchovsky**
**Mazeh Street, Tel Aviv**
**March 2011**

**INTRODUCTION**

**Anat Rosenberg**

Tel Aviv has come a long way since its modest start in 1909, when 66 pioneering Zionist families stood on a sand dune on the outskirts of Jaffa to parcel out plots of land that together would form the fledgling Ahuzat Bayit ("Homestead"). Of course, some neighborhoods like Neve Tzedek and Kerem Hateimanim that currently are part of Tel Aviv existed well before that watershed year, but it's mind-boggling to think that so much of what we see here today—just two years after the city celebrated its centennial—simply wasn't around back then. When looking at Tel Aviv and walking around it, soaking up its rich offerings, it's equally mind-boggling to think of all that has been built and created, achieved and accomplished in this relatively young city, whose name, meaning "Hill of Spring," was taken from the Hebrew title of Theodore Herzl's visionary Zionist work *Altneuland*.

In a sense, a modified, modernized version of that pioneering spirit courses through Tel Avivians' veins today: Everywhere you look in the city, there are dozens of cranes towering overhead and corrugated steel construction fences signaling that the building frenzy still endures. Thankfully, though, much of the city's beautiful Eclectic and International-style architecture is being preserved as a result of city bylaws that mandate conservation of architecturally notable and historic structures. Everywhere you go, you see evidence of non-stop intellectual and business pursuits and prolific artistic creation. This small strip of land—which measures approximately 51 square kilometers, or about 20 square miles, and is home to more than 404,000 people—is Israel's economic and cultural hub, and its aspirations are only growing bigger.

In 2011, the municipality launched TLV Global City, a national initiative aimed at elevating Tel Aviv-Jaffa's status to what is known as a global city, an urban center with significant international standing based on its financial, social and cultural activity. The municipality's goal is for Tel Aviv to have achieved this status within a decade, and in order to fulfill that goal it is attracting international financial institutions and corporations that will help transform the city into a global economic force; and it is working to make Tel Aviv's unique cultural assets, its local DNA, more accessible to global markets. Just some of what the municipality has planned as part of this effort is a year-long art celebration to mark the opening of the new Tel Aviv Museum of Art building; the establishment of fixed dates for three of the city's most popular events (White Night, the marathon and the Gay Pride Parade) that have broad international appeal; the creation of an Israeli Heritage Mile within the city that will weave through its historic parts, including Bialik Street, Rothschild Boulevard and Jaffa; and the upkeep of the beachfront in accordance with international standards.

All of these proposals are sure to increase Tel Aviv's appeal, but the city already has plenty to offer, and what makes it a hot spot (and not just because it lies at the center of a volatile region, or because of its unlimited WiFi) is its uninhibited love—or lust—for life. And not just life, but the best possible life, the kind that is lived to the fullest at every waking moment and makes use of all of one's senses.

There's no denying that Tel Aviv lives up to its reputation for being a bubble, for being more than a little detached from the reality surrounding it, for cultivating a mentality that could be described as "work hard, play harder." While that reputation has been somewhat problematic for Tel Aviv residents, mostly left-wing and center-left liberals within an increasingly right-leaning country, it also has helped to attract an increasing number of visitors from abroad, who come here looking to take advantage of the city's 24/7 atmosphere and boundless energy.

Tel Aviv is home to first-rate culture, including dozens of galleries, museums and architectural landmarks recognized by UNESCO as a World Heritage Site; it is also home to numerous historic spots, many of which are in Jaffa; more than a dozen theaters, a number of which feature productions with subtitles in other languages; music venues that stage performances in multiple genres; green parks and gardens; chic cafés; stylish boutiques with truly innovative fashion; great vintage shopping; sizzling beaches; trendy boutique hotels; a thriving LGBT scene; a spirited bar and nightlife scene; eye-catching graffiti; and world-class restaurants that fuse top-notch ingredients, including fresh and flavorful locally grown produce, with an array of other cultures and cuisines.

Tel Aviv is not one of those cities that come alive only on the weekend: On any given day or night, there are gallery openings and concerts, lectures and theater performances, yoga and spinning classes along the promenade or at the port, design fairs and flea markets, food festivals, political protests and street parties. Cafés are perpetually full, the beach is crowded with sunbathers and surfers, the boulevards are filled with people strolling, riding bikes or relaxing on a bench—so much so that you sometimes wonder if anyone actually works around here. The city thrives on the unexpected, the spontaneous, the ephemeral. Boutiques, bars and restaurants that are super trendy one minute are shuttered the next. Alas, even some of the places the last edition of *City Guide Tel Aviv* wrote about enthusiastically are no longer with us. New places pop up and disappear, and it's all part of the rhythm and cycle of life here, seemingly more so than in other cities.

That spontaneity is an inherent part of the mentality in Tel Aviv—and it extends to all aspects of life, from keeping track of time to making plans with friends or family to the street-food culture of falafel and hummus. (The only exception to this rule is dinner

reservations, which are a must on any given night at all worthwhile restaurants.) One thing foreigners tend to notice early on about locals is that they don't make plans in advance, and they might even look at you funny if you ask them on a Monday what their plans are for the weekend. Many Tel Avivians, for whatever reason, don't like to feel locked in to specific plans ahead of time. One of their favorite verbs is "leezrom," meaning to flow, and they will often use it or a variation on it with guests to tell them to relax, be flexible, take it easy. After a while, you simply adjust and realize that the rhythm here is what you make it.

Compared with other cities, Tel Aviv might not be the prettiest or the cleanest, and on some days it feels more developing than developed, but in some ways that is part of its appeal—it doesn't try to whitewash its flaws. The principal source of joy in Tel Aviv is found in the simple pleasures: a leisurely stroll or bicycle ride from Tel Aviv to Jaffa; lingering over a coffee and snack at one of the many cafés around town; gazing out at the Mediterranean from the beachfront; the stray cats (if you're an animal lover); the smell of jasmine or honeysuckle that wafts by out of nowhere; the sense of personal safety, even at late hours of the night. These are the things that make Tel Aviv unique, and we hope you enjoy our city's simple pleasures as much as we do.

**Now, here are some things to know for getting here and around:**

- **There is a fixed daytime taxi rate** of approximately NIS 130 from Ben-Gurion International Airport, about a 20 minutes' drive with no traffic, to central Tel Aviv. This fare includes one suitcase per passenger, and additional suitcases are about NIS 4 each. The rate will be higher after 9 p.m. and from sundown Friday to sundown Saturday.

- **Trains** travel between Ben-Gurion International Airport and the Arlozorov (Savidor), Hashalom and Hagana stations once or twice an hour, 24 hours a day. Tickets cost approximately NIS 15, and schedules can be seen here: www.rail.co.il.

- **Tel Aviv is compact and fairly walkable**, but public transportation is plentiful:
  - **Taxis abound**, and while drivers sometimes see tourists as soft targets, they are required by law to turn on the meter ("moneh" is Hebrew). It is not customary to tip taxi drivers.
  - **The two main bus companies**, Dan and Egged, run numerous lines within the city and from Tel Aviv elsewhere. Check www.dan.co.il and www.egged.co.il for schedules. The adult fare in Tel Aviv is NIS 6.
  - **Ten-passenger yellow minivans**, known individually as a "sherut," pick up and drop off anywhere you like along their routes, and generally cost about one shekel more than regular buses.

**More useful information:**

- **The country code** for Israel is +972, while the local area code, in most cases, is (03).

- **Tipping** at restaurants and cafés is the standard 15 percent, and is generally left in cash even if the bill is paid by credit card.

- **Most businesses close on Friday afternoon and re-open Sunday morning.** Restaurants, cafés, kiosks, bars, cinemas and clubs are generally open over the weekend, but there are always exceptions, so check before going out.

- **Eating well** in Tel Aviv is never an issue: Most cafés, including the big chains, serve reasonably priced fresh salads and sandwiches, and most places offer a variety of vegetarian options.

- **Dress in Tel Aviv** is extremely casual, and "dressed up" generally means upscale casual. Suits, with the exception of business meetings, are practically unheard of here. Good style, as in any major city, is always appreciated.

- **Tel Aviv is sunny on most days of the year.** Winters are short and sometimes rainy, while summers are uncomfortably hot and humid. Don't forget to apply sunscreen and drink a lot of water—the sun here can be brutal.

- And, finally, **a quick note about the locals**: Tel Avivians are honest to a fault and don't mince words, which might be off-putting at first, but you get used to having opinions about everything tossed your way, often unsolicited. Israelis have a reputation for lacking the manners and finesse found elsewhere, and for being pushy and little rough around the edges—but, on the flip side, when they warm up to you, it is genuine and their embrace is usually full-force and nearly unconditional.

Jerusalem

Hamasger

Menachem Begin

Rival
Yad Harutzim
Harakevet
Hatzfira

Yad Harutzim

Neve Sha'anan

Har Zion Blvd

Levinsky
Wolfson

Albert Square
Nachmani
Bezalel Yafe
Mazeh
Shadal
Yavne
Gan Hashmal
Hahashmal
Barzilay
Levontin
Hatashbetz

SOUTH

Allenby
Nahalat Binyamin
Shefer
Montefiore
Montefiore
Lilienblum
Hetchal
Haalmud
Derech Yafo

Herzl
Matalon
Frenkel
Florentin
Washington Blvd
Vital
Abarbanel
Alfasi

Ben Zvi

Shalom Tower

Ha Carmel Market

Neve Zedek
Ein Ya'akov
Achva
Shabazi
Yechieli
Chelouche
Suzanne Dallal Center
Elifelet
Eilat
American Colony
Kibbutz Galuyot
Noga

Jerusalem Blvd

Arkon

Koifman

Hatachana Complex

Tirza
Nechama
Salame

Ben Yair
Yoezer
Flea Market
Olei Zion
Yochanan
Hachubit
Hapninim

Yehuda Margoza
Yehuda Hayamit
Shivtei Israel

Beach

The Dolphinarium

Alma Beach

Old Jaffa
Hatzorfim
Pasteur

Yefet
Yefet

JAFFA
Ajami
Kedem

Toulouse

Hadolphin

Jaffa Port

The heart • Le Cœur

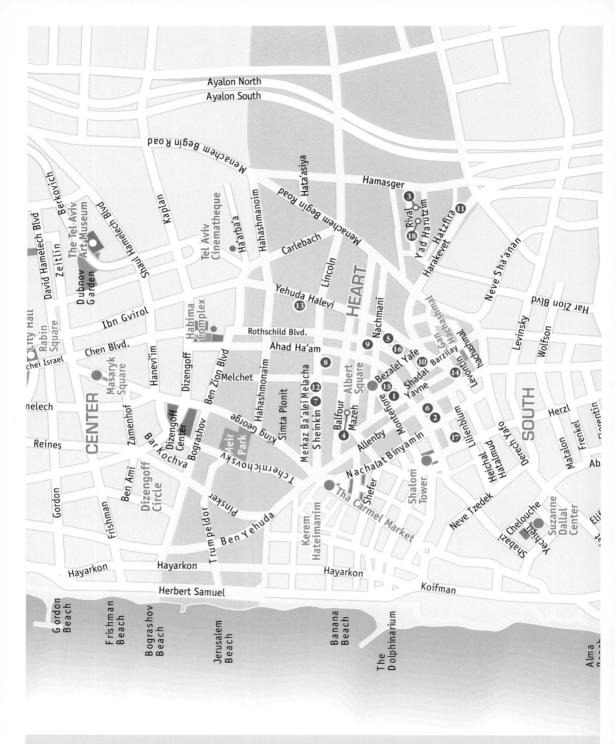

Ayalon North
Ayalon South

Menachem Begin Road

Hamasger

Hata'asiya

Menachem Begin Road

Kaplan

Berkovich

David Hamelech Blvd
Zeitlin

Shaul Hamelech Blvd

The Tel Aviv
Art Museum

Dubnov
Garden

Ha'arba'a

Hahashmanoim

Carlebach

Tel Aviv
Cinematheque

**③**
Rival
**⑱**

Yad Harutzim

Harakevet

Hatzfira

**⑪**

Neve Sha'anan

Lincoln

Yehuda Halevi

**⑬**

**HEART**

Nachmani

Hachashmal

Gan Hachashmal

Har Zion Blvd

Levinsky
Wolfson

Ibn Gvirol

City Hall
Rabin
Square

rchei Israel

Chen Blvd.

Habima
Complex

Rothschild Blvd.

Ahad Ha'am

**⑨**

**⑤**

Bezalel Yafe

**⑯**

**⑩**

Shadal

Levontin

Barzilay

**⑭**

Hanevi'im

Masaryk
Square

Dizengoff

Ben Zion Blvd

Melchet

Hahashmonaim

**⑧**

Albert
Square

**①**

Yavne

**⑥**

**②**

**SOUTH**

Herzl

nelech

Reines

**CENTER**

Zamenhof

Bar Kochva

Dizengoff
Center

Bograshov

King George

Simta Plonit

**⑫**

Merkaz Ba'alei Melacha

Sheinkin

**⑦**

Balfour

Mazeh

**④**

**⑮**

Montefiore

Yavne

Nachalat Binyamin

**⑰**

Lilienblum

Heichal
Hatalmud

Frenkel
Matalon

Ab

Gordon

Ben Ami

Dizengoff
Circle

Pinsker

Tchernichovsky

Meir
Park

Ben Yehuda

Shefer

Nachalat Binyamin

Shalom
Tower

Neve Tzedek

Derech Yafo

Frishman

Trumpeldor

Kerem
Hateimanim

Tha Carmel Market

Neve Tzedek

Chelouche

Shabazi

Yechiel

Suzanne
Dallal
Center

Elif

Hayarkon

Hayarkon

Hayarkon

Koifman

Herbert Samuel

Gordon
Beach

Frishman
Beach

Bograshov
Beach

Jerusalem
Beach

Banana
Beach

The
Dolphinarium

Alma

# The Heart • Le Cœur

The sections of Tel Aviv that form its "heart" are indeed the vital core of the city that pumps energy into the surrounding streets, which are generally abuzz with life no matter the hour. The heart extends from Ben Zion Boulevard in the north to Allenby Street in the south, and its central artery is the grand, tree-lined Rothschild Boulevard—one of the earliest streets to have been built in Tel Aviv after its establishment in 1909 that today is one of its most popular and dynamic. The area called the heart contains a number of structures that are integral parts of Tel Aviv history, including a handful of small museums, some of the country's most remarkable synagogues, a number of quirky Eclectic-style buildings and a wealth of the International-style architecture for which Tel Aviv garnered its reputation as the White City.

Yet for all the history here, the heart is an utterly modern, thriving area that is part sleek business district, part booming entertainment and cultural center, part posh residential neighborhood. This is the center of Israeli commerce where the Tel Aviv Stock Exchange and branches of top investment banks and law firms sit comfortably next to some of the city's finest art galleries and trendiest nightlife hot spots. This part of Tel Aviv also offers visitors cutting-edge shopping, quality restaurants and cafés and plenty of scenic streets to stroll. It contains some of the most desirable property in Tel Aviv, and is where (to the praise of some and the dismay of others) a 32-story tower designed by architect Richard Meier, scheduled for completion in 2013, will reside alongside some of the city's Bauhaus landmarks. The heart's diversity applies not only to its attractions, but also to its social composition: It's not uncommon to see Hasidic Jews crossing paths with tattooed and pierced twenty-somethings in a somewhat surreal manifestation of the city's "live and let live" attitude.

## Rothschild Boulevard

Named after benefactor Baron Edmond James de Rothschild, this expansive boulevard plays a pivotal role in Tel Aviv's urban fabric, especially in the stretch within the heart of the city. By far one of Tel Aviv's most picturesque streets, the boulevard—which runs from Habima Theatre in the north to the edge of Neve Tzedek in the south—is shaded by enormous ficus trees and lined with benches that are frequented day and night. That boundless energy is clearly a large part of Rothschild's appeal: It manages to remain vibrant

without feeling frenetic, busy but never claustrophobic. The boulevard is one of Tel Aviv's main destinations for a laid-back walk or bike ride, and on any given day there you might encounter a temporary art installation, a busker performing or a tarot-card reader waiting to divine your future. Rothschild is also home to a number of restaurants, cafés (some open around the clock) and bars, as well as coffee kiosks along the boulevard itself, where locals often sit with their morning coffee and read the newspaper or young couples pushing strollers gather with friends for a leisurely chat.

## Yehuda Halevi Street

Yehuda Halevi runs parallel to Rothschild Boulevard, and while the street lacks its neighbor's splendor, its gentrification over the last decade has brought with it a subdued aura of cool. There are a number of friendly, low-key cafés here, as well as a couple of trendy bars and restaurants that are mainstays for local artists and hipsters. In recent years, a handful of art galleries have migrated to Yehuda Halevi, and stores carrying specialty housewares and funky furniture have moved in as well.

## Shadal Street

Shadal Street, which connects Yehuda Halevi with Rothschild Boulevard, is small in size but big on architectural treasures, including some beautifully refurbished heritage houses and the famous Ohel Moed synagogue. Inaugurated in 1931, the Sephardic house of worship favored in the past by some of Tel Aviv's elite is renowned for its splendid domed roof and remains a popular spot for weddings.

## Gan Hahashmal

Just a few minutes' walk from Shadal Street is the Gan Hahashmal neighborhood, which takes its name ("Electric Garden" in Hebrew) from Tel Aviv's first power plant. The district has weathered several incarnations since its early days: During the 1940s it was a bustling area that fell into disrepair after the power plant closed in the 1970s, and it was considered one of the seedier parts of Tel Aviv into the '90s. But the small park at the center of the neighborhood, and the streets surrounding it, have recovered in recent years thanks to their rediscovery by the local fashion crowd and a little municipal upkeep. Small boutiques here carry fashion and accessories from some of Israel's homegrown talents, and the area is also home to Levontin 7, one of Tel Aviv's most popular live-music venues, a cozy yoga studio offering Ashtanga and Vinyasa classes for all levels, as well as several cool cafés.

Historic City Hall Building

## Ahad Ha'am Street

Ahad Ha'am Street, which runs parallel to Rothschild Boulevard, is one of the longest and most important streets in the heart of the city, both architecturally and historically. It is named after Asher Ginsberg, the Hebrew essayist considered the founder of cultural Zionism who was more commonly known by his pen name Ahad Ha'am ("one of the people") and who lived on this street until his death in 1927. Some beautifully renovated International-style buildings can be found along Ahad Ha'am, while its southern end near Neve Tzedek is home to some of Tel Aviv's oldest Eclectic-style structures.

Nearby Montefiore Street is another architecturally distinguished street that leads to one of Tel Aviv's most unique and beautiful landmarks. Located at the corner of Nachmani Street, the Pagoda House, constructed in 1924 and renovated in the late 1990s, features pillars, arches and other decorative elements that join east and west in a fusion that can't be found elsewhere in the city. It was also the first building in Tel Aviv to have an elevator for domestic use.

At the foot of Pagoda House lies the enchanting King Albert Square, named after King Albert the First of Belgium, who visited Tel Aviv in 1933. This little oasis, with its two towering ficus trees and a shaded bench, is without a doubt one of the most peaceful places in the city.

## Sheinkin Street

Sheinkin Street, considered by some to be Tel Aviv's equivalent to Greenwich Village, was actually part of an aging neighborhood built in the early 20th century that began to deteriorate in the 1950s. Sheinkin experienced a turning point in the 1980s, when it developed into a bastion of Tel Aviv bohemia: Artists, writers, musicians and actors all took up residence here and transformed the street into a hub for left-wing, alternative culture. The municipality also supported Sheinkin's resurgence by aiding in the overhaul of some of its crumbling buildings and giving the park that now houses a community center a much-needed facelift. During the street's heyday, it became something of a rite of passage for teenagers to stroll and shop on Sheinkin, especially on Friday mornings when, even today, visitors crowd the street and its cafés. Now, however, fancy brand-name stores such as Adidas and Diesel have replaced many of Shenkin's eccentric, independent shops, and the street isn't quite as avant garde as it was a decade or two ago. Sheinkin is still worth a

visit, though, if only to catch a glimpse of its past at such legendary spots as Café Tamar, the no-frills establishment run for decades by proprietress Sara Stern, who livens up the place with her chitchat and often-heated discussions.

**King George Street** Named after George V, who ruled the United Kingdom during the British Mandate era, King George Street is one of the busiest thoroughfares in the heart of the city, making it a great place for people watching. King George south of Ben Zion Boulevard is a mish-mash of cheap clothing stores, cafés, bakeries, second-hand book and jewelry stores and other random shops. At its southern end, King George leads to Magen David Square, where Allenby Street, the Carmel Market, Nahalat Binyamin and Sheinkin Street all meet at what is arguably the most hectic intersection in Tel Aviv. Just off King George is Bezalel Market, where locals go to rummage through piles of clothing, swimwear and accessories at bargain prices, and then have a snack at the neighboring falafel stand.

**Simta Almonit and Simta Plonit** Also in the King George vicinity are two quaint alleys called Simta Almonit and Simta Plonit ("Anonymous Alley" and "So-and-So Alley," respectively) that sit parallel to one another. Local legend has it that Meir Dizengoff, the city's first mayor, gave the streets their unusual names after an argument with their founder, who wanted to name them after himself and his wife. Today, Almonit and Plonit are better known for their pleasant cafés, a number of which have outdoor garden seating as well as number of top-notch second-hand clothing shops.

**Gan Meir** For a break from all the activity along King George, step into Meir Park, located between King George and Tchernichovsky Streets south of Dizengoff Center. This refuge from the surrounding gritty urban landscape contains bench-lined, tree-shaded paths, along with a fish pond, playground and one of the most widely used dog runs around. The park is also home to Tel Aviv's LGBT community center, and the café adjacent to it feels like one of the best-kept secrets in the city.

**Bialik Street** Tucked away just off the hustle and bustle of Allenby Street is Bialik Street, a small but charming street that blends International and Eclectic buildings, some of which are valuable

Top: Historical Russian Embassy Building, Rothschild Blvd.

**Rising**, Menashe Kadishman, 1974, Habima Sq.

components of Tel Aviv's cultural and architectural history. The street is named after Israel's national poet, Haim Nahman Bialik, and his former home, now a museum, is just one of the structures along this short strip to have benefited from the city's preservation efforts. Recently refurbished to restore its original appearance, the house contains Bialik's books and personal objects along with artworks given to him by a number of his contemporaries. There are three other museums along this street that combined make for an afternoon well-spent: Beit Ha'ir ("Town Hall"), the beautifully renovated building overlooking Bialik Square that served as Tel Aviv's first city hall and now offers exhibitions on local history; the Rubin Museum, which chronicles the life and work of Reuven Rubin, a celebrated Israeli painter; and the Bauhaus Foundation Museum, a private home that was also renovated several years ago to display furniture, photography and other works by seminal designers including Mies van der Rohe and Marcel Breuer.

## Trumpeldor Cemetery

Another notable place that is well worth visiting is Trumpeldor Cemetery. Founded in 1902, this is the final resting place of some of the country's leading historical, cultural and political dignitaries. Bialik, Meir Dizengoff, Shaul Tchernichovsky and Ahad Ha'am are all buried in this veritable pantheon, along with additional figures whose names grace the streets of Tel Aviv and other Israeli cities.

*Hotel • Hôtel*

*Restaurant • Restaurant*

# HOTEL MONTEFIORE
36 Montefiore St.
Tel. (03) 564 6100
www.hotelmontefiore.co.il
*Map/Carte 1*

# HOTEL MONTEFIORE RESTAURANT & BAR
36 Montefiore St.
Tel. (03) 564 6100
www.hotelmontefiore.co.il
*Map/Carte 1*

Hotel Montefiore resides in a beautifully restored 1920s Eclectic-style building, and its salmon-hued façade stands out even in the heart of the White City. The hotel contains 12 meticulously designed, well-appointed rooms that feature sleek furnishings and cutting-edge technology. Each of the rooms also provides a touch of culture, including a library with titles in multiple languages and works by local artists. Hotel Montefiore prides itself on uncompromisingly professional service and its welcoming staff makes guests feel like family. Tel Aviv has witnessed a fresh crop of boutique hotels open in recent years, but Hotel Montefiore is the one that started the trend— and it remains the gold standard in terms of luxury accommodation and impeccable service.

Located on the ground floor, Hotel Montefiore's restaurant serves Vietnamese-influenced brasserie cuisine in stylishly elegant surroundings. Unlike many hotel restaurants, the Montefiore's is an attraction in and of itself: Trendy locals and well-to-do business types are among the worldly clientele that flocks here to enjoy lavish breakfasts or flavorful main dishes, including tuna sashimi, refreshing spring rolls, crispy chicken and Tom Yom seafood casserole. The restaurant also serves afternoon tea with scones, while the bar offers afternoon cocktails and heats up at night when the sexy, fabulous crowd takes over.

# DANIELLA LEHAVI

21 Rothschild Blvd.
Tel. (03) 629 4044
34 Basel St.
Tel. (03) 544 0573
www.daniellalehavi.com
*Map/Carte 2*

Swiss-born designer Daniella Lehavi pioneered the concept of the designer handbag in Israel when she opened her studio in 1990. Lehavi's first, modest collection included only ten bags; since then, her collections not only have grown to include wallets, belts and shoes, but her name has come to symbolize elegant, custom-made accessories crafted from the highest-quality leather. Fashionable Israeli women have long swooned for Lehavi's products, which are chic and modern, and effortlessly merge form and function. Lehavi is especially attentive to detail in her designs and carefully considers the division of compartments, length of straps and placement of zippers to ensure maximum comfort and convenience. Her Tel Aviv boutiques feature minimalist décor that allows the wares to stand out, and the outgoing staff is always happy to help you choose just the right accessory to spruce up your wardrobe.

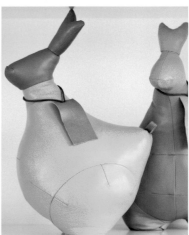

*Café • Café*

## BAKERY

13 Yad Harutzim St.
Tel. (03) 537 1041
www.bakerytlv.co.il
*Map/Carte 3*

Nestled next to door to the ever-popular Coffee
Bar, this original branch of Bakery may be
surrounded by auto body shops in the industrial
Yad Harutzim neighborhood, but it feels as though
it were transplanted from France. This gem of a
café has for years catered to carbohydrate-loving
residents of Tel Aviv, who are happy to make a
short pilgrimage in order to indulge in Bakery's
flaky croissants, berry-filled pastries, golden
muffins and brioches, quiches and other decadent
cakes. Bakery also caters to the local lunch crowd,
and offers hearty sandwiches featuring chicken
breast, roast beef or the Coffee Bar's ever-popular
schnitzel on gourmet breads or baguettes.
Healthier options include a spicy carrot salad,
pasta salad and quinoa salad. There are a few
marble-topped tables at the entrance, where you
can feel like a local while enjoying a breakfast
pastry or sandwich along with your perfectly
prepared coffee.

# BOOKWORM

7 Mazeh St.
Tel. (03) 535 7038
www.bookworm.co.il
*Map/Carte 4*

Fans of Bookworm, the legendary shop near Rabin Square, rejoiced last year when owners Eliana Ydov and Fanny Hershenzon decided to open another branch in a beautifully renovated Eclectic-style building in the heart of Tel Aviv. Designed in the 1920s by architect Joseph Berlin, the spectacular structure known locally as the Twin House provides an ideal setting for the cozy bookstore-café. Bookworm shares the space with a contemporary art gallery, and this branch, fittingly, places a stronger emphasis on art, architecture, photography and design titles. The menu here includes omelettes, salads, sandwiches and sweets—perfect for snacking on while contemplating art and life.

---

*Art • Art*

## HIBINO
30 Yavne St. • Tel. (03) 516 0352

Meaning "daily" in Japanese, Hibino re-creates the spirit of Japan in Israel through Japanese art, crafts, interior design housewares and everyday items showcased in a space that is both enriching and inspiring.

*Restaurant • Restaurant*

## CAFÉ NOIR
43 Ahad Ha'am St. • Tel. (03) 566 3018

This bistro is a Tel Aviv institution that remains popular for its elegantly relaxed ambience and top-notch food, including its celebrated schnitzel, widely considered the best in the city.

*Concept store • Magasin spécialisé*

## SABON
28 Sheinkin St. • Tel. (03) 558 6740

Sabon returned to Sheinkin Street, where it got its start in 1997, with a new concept store offering visitors the ultimate pampering experience. This internationally successful beauty emporium is renowned for its soaps sold by weight, rich body lotions, hand creams, exfoliating scrubs and more made from the finest ingredients.

*Design • Design*

## CAROUSELLA
81 Yehuda Halevi St. • Tel. (03) 560 3750

This high-end contemporary design house offers colorful, fun and creative furnishings and accessories for children's bedrooms, most of which are manufactured in Israel.

*Night • Nuit*

## BREAKFAST CLUB
6 Rothschild Blvd.

Stealth stairs lead to this dim basement bar-club along southern Rothschild Boulevard. The Breakfast Club is legendary for its raucous parties that only start to heat up around 3 a.m. By the time you leave, you'll be ready for a good breakfast.

*Fashion • Mode*

## MOR VE YOS
13 Barzilay St. • Tel. (077) 322 3375

Mor Hemed and Yossi Malca are two graduates of the Bezalel Academy of Arts and Design who joined forces to create a house of design, fashion and lovely leather handbags and accessories.

*Restaurant • Restaurant*

## JOZ VE LOZ
51 Yehuda Halevi St. • Tel. (03) 560 6385

Considered one of the hippest hangouts in the city, this funky restaurant is renowned for its flea-market décor, menu that changes daily, art world and celebrity patrons and apathetic service.

*Night • Nuit*

## PAR DERRIÈRE
4 King George St. • Tel. (03) 629 2111

A romantic wine bar tucked away in a magical garden courtyard located just off King George Street, Par Derrière offers a wide selection of wines and small bites.

*Night • Nuit*

## MILK
6 Rothschild Blvd.

Milk is the Breakfast Club's younger, somewhat rebellious sibling, designed in the form of an apartment with all the appropriate rooms and fixtures. The vibe and the people are youthful and hip, especially at the regular Friday night party, Misshapes, co-hosted by Milk and the Breakfast Club.

# SARIT SHANI HAY

36 Nachmani St.
Tel. (03) 566 6987
www.shanihay.com
*Map/Carte 5*

Tucked away in an unassuming building in the heart of Tel Aviv is the showroom and studio of Sarit Shani Hay, one of Israel's leading interior, furniture and toy designers. Stepping inside Sarit Shani Hay is like entering a colorful, imaginative wonderland that celebrates playful living for both children and adults. The showroom displays Shani Hay's unique designs for bedrooms for children, teens and adults, which are characterized by clean, modern lines, vivid color palettes and a dose of humor. Shani Hay draws inspiration from comic books, fairy tales, modernist design and African art, and she works with an equally diverse range of materials to create functional yet fun pieces. Her studio offers comprehensive interior design services, along with custom furniture and accessories. Shani Hay's work has been featured in the international press, and she has also been commissioned to work on projects in schools, libraries and children's hospitals across Israel.

## BENEDICT BLVD.

29 Rothschild Blvd.
Tel. (03) 686 8657
*Map/Carte 6*

## BENEDICT

171 Ben Yehuda St.
Tel. (03) 544 0345

They say that breakfast is the most important meal of the day, and at Benedict, breakfast isn't simply a meal, it's a way of life. The restaurant's groundbreaking concept is to serve up breakfast in a variety of incarnations 24 hours a day, seven days a week—and it's been doing just that since the launch of its first restaurant on Ben Yehuda Street in 2006. This location, tucked away on the corner of Jabotinsky Street, combines classic European-style café with hints of an upscale American diner, while the Rothschild restaurant brings these stylish settings to the heart of Tel Aviv. Benedict's creative menu blends a variety of flavors and breakfast options from different cultures around the world. There are numerous savory options, including traditional eggs Benedict and Florentine; decadent steak and eggs; eggs served with crispy bacon or juicy ham; traditional Mediterranean breakfast options, including salads and shakshuka; and Benedict's own invention, "egg balls," which resemble gnocchi and are served in different sauces. Benedict also offers mouth-watering pancakes, with blueberries or chocolate, and buttery French toast made with brioche bread that is baked on premises. No matter the hour, Benedict's professional and courteous staff always greets diners with a hearty "Good morning!"

Make Time For Breakfast

## Hollandaise Sauce

1 gr. cracked black peppercorns    270 ml. melt
45 ml. white wine vinegar         7 ml. lemon
45 ml. water                      salt as nee
4 egg yolks

# ORNA AND ELLA
33 Sheinkin St.
Tel. (03) 620 4753
*Map/Carte* **7**

This understated restaurant nestled among the boutiques of Sheinkin Street began as a neighborhood café that has grown into a Tel Aviv institution. Orna and Ella prides itself on simplicity, as evidenced by the stark white space (with no background music) that leaves the focus on the food—all of which is made on premises using the freshest ingredients straight from the market. Everything on the menu—including the crisp salads, handmade pastas, inventive fish and meat courses and tasty sweets—is flavorful and delicious. Whatever you order, make sure to try the sweet potato pancakes, which are justifiably legendary.

## MOSES
35 Rothschild Blvd. • Tel. *9499

This family-friendly bar and grill overlooking Rothschild Boulevard has an extensive menu of updated American classics, like juicy burgers with various toppings and charbroiled chicken, along with local favorites including an extra-crispy schnitzel.

## CAFÉ TACHTIT
9 Lincoln St. • Tel. (03) 561 8759

Despite a location that's a little out of the way, this cozy café with outdoor seating attracts much of Tel Aviv's artsy, bohemian crowd.

## SHAMPINA
32 Rothschild Blvd. • Tel. (03) 560 8852

Shampina calls itself a "sparkling bar," and true to its name, it offers champagne, cava and other bubbly drinks in an equally bubbly atmosphere.

## CAFÉ TAMAR
57 Sheinkin St. • Tel. (03) 685 2376

Judging by the Formica tables and plastic chairs, you might not have guessed that Café Tamar is legendary in Tel Aviv. It was once the hub of Tel Aviv's intellectual bohemian scene, and it's definitely worth a visit if only to catch a glimpse of its feisty owner Sara Stern.

## CAFÉ NOAH
93 Ahad Ha'am St. • Tel. (03) 629 3799

Perched on a quiet corner in the heart of Tel Aviv, Noah has a charming little patio and book-lined interior, and is popular with writers and artists.

## VA'AD HABAYIT
64 Rothschild Blvd.

This enormously popular neighborhood bar is set in a stunning old building along Rothschild Boulevard. The crowd, often dressed to the nines with bling included, is equally beautiful.

## CAFÉ ITALIA
6 Kreminitzky St. • Tel. (03) 561 2888

Modeled after traditional trattorias and ristorantes, this vibrant eatery serves up wonderfully flavorful Italian classics.

## FRAU BLAU
8 Hahashmal St. • Tel. (03) 560 1735

Named for owners Helena Blaunstein and Phillip Blau, this colorful boutique stocks their avant-garde, whimsical fashions for women.

## PASTA MIA
10 Wilson St. • Tel. (03) 561 0189

Pasta Mia is a cozy Italian restaurant that serves traditional fare, including bruschetta, caprese salad and homemade pasta, with your choice of sauce. Their fresh pasta is also available for sale by weight.

# STORY

60 Sheinkin St.
Tel. (03) 560 3911
*Map/Carte 8*

Sheinkin Street is lined with shops selling upscale brands, urban streetwear, trendy footwear and accessories, but none offers the exciting blend of brands that make up Story. Like its sister store on Dizengoff, the Story boutique in the heart of Tel Aviv presents an innovative approach to shopping by offering apparel, footwear and accessories, with equal consideration given to men and women. The boutiques' umbrella group, 911 Fashion, holds exclusive import and distribution rights to a number of international brands and believes that each brand has a story (hence the name); it carefully selects the best individual pieces from each brand to create a coherent collection for Story, a one-stop multi-brand shop. Among the favorites that can be found here are Melissa's multicolored plastic shoes, Nudie Jeans, Fornarina, Fly London shoes, along with some top Israeli designers.

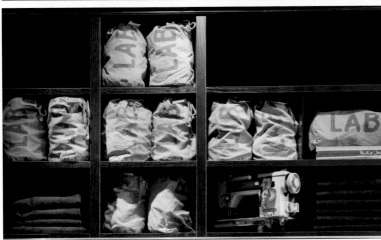

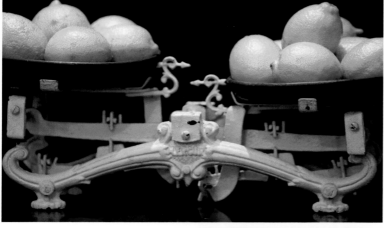

# ROTHSCHILD'S KITCHEN
73 Rothschild Blvd.
Tel. (03) 525 7171
*Map/Carte* **9**

Situated on one of the most vibrant corners in the heart of the city, Rothschild's Kitchen offers diners modern bistro fare in a dynamic urban setting that still manages to exude warmth. Patrons can choose between the restaurant's indoor seating area—which features casually elegant décor and large windows facing the leafy and lively Rothschild Boulevard—and the outdoor patio area, which is at the center of the boulevard's action and is a great spot for an after-work cocktail. The diverse menu, meanwhile, includes original takes on classic bistro options and courses that fuse Mediterranean and European influences. Some of the highlights include a sirloin steak served with creamy mashed potatoes, a spicy Moroccan fish course, a seafood trio in an herb broth and decadent homemade desserts. Like the boulevard for which it's named, Rothschild's Kitchen buzzes with life both day and night.

# RADIO E.P.G.B.

7 Shadal St.
Tel. (03) 560 3636
www.radioepgb.com
*Map/Carte* 10

Tucked away next to an old synagogue on Shadal Street, Radio E.P.G.B. caters to worshippers of a different kind: those who adore all the elements that combine to create top-notch nightlife. Radio E.P.G.B. garnered a reputation for its music, and it consistently showcases the hottest indie and electronic DJs in town and hosts live performances. But the glam rock club/bar is equally renowned for attracting in-the-know patrons oozing incredible style, and for the overall buzz felt inside (and even in the long lines frequently seen outside). Radio E.P.G.B. is one of the most unique places to experience Tel Aviv nightlife, and that's saying a lot for a city that has its fair share of night owls.

## *Fashion • Mode*

### ALMA
9 Merkaz Ba'alei Melacha St. • Tel. (03) 620 0145

Long considered one of Tel Aviv's super-stylish boutiques, Alma is the perfect choice for the trendy urban woman.

## *Restaurant • Restaurant*

### HASALON
8 Ma'avar Hayavok St. • Tel. (052) 703 5888

The brainchild of celebrity Chef Eyal Shani, this exclusive restaurant located in a remote part of Tel Aviv is only open Wednesdays and Thursdays, and serves a constantly changing menu using the freshest local ingredients. Worth the schlep and the splurge.

## *Café • Café*

### DINITZ
22 Nahalat Binyamin St. • Tel. (03) 510 4665

This veteran café-bakery renowned for its European feel and attractive waitstaff recently relocated to a historic building along Nahalat Binyamin.

## *Restaurant • Restaurant*

### STEFAN BRAUN
99 Allenby St. • Tel. (03) 560 4725

Tucked away in a picturesque old courtyard set back from noisy Allenby Street, Stefan Braun serves tasty Middle Eastern appetizers and meat dishes in a relaxed Ottoman-era setting.

## *Café • Café*

### NECHAMA VAHETZI
144 Ahad Ha'am St. • Tel. (03) 685 2326

Perched on the corner opposite Habima Theatre, this charming neighborhood café features a lovely outdoor patio, and serves up tasty salads, sandwiches and pastas—along with alcohol at rock-bottom prices.

## *Hotel • Hôtel*

### SEA EXECUTIVE SUITES
76 Herbert Samuel St. • Tel. (03) 795 3434

This elegant boutique hotel facing the beach provides tourists and business travelers alike top-tier amenities and excellent service.

## *Books • Livres*

### HAMIGDALOR
4 Harakevet St. • Tel. (03) 686 8225

Meaning "lighthouse" in Hebrew, Hamigdalor is a new bookstore and gift shop that prides itself on its independent spirit.

## *Design • Design*

### PRIMITIVE
77 Yehuda Halevi St. • Tel. (03) 566 0551

Primitive is a beautiful showroom featuring an eclectic mix of ethnic designs, modern furniture, primitive objects and tribal and contemporary art. The space also hosts changing art and design exhibitions.

## *Beauty • Beauté*

### FOXY SALON
85 Yehuda Halevi St. • Tel. (03) 566 2050

Foxy Salon's goal is to provide clients with an extensive array of the most pampering beauty treatments using the best brands, all under one roof in central Tel Aviv.

# CUCINA TAMAR

10 Hatzfira St.
Tel. (03) 639 0407
www.rest.co.il/cucina_tamar
*Map/Carte 11*

Located on a somewhat desolate street in the Yad Harutzim neighborhood, Cucina Tamar is an Italian oasis that serves imaginative dishes in sophisticated yet laid-back surroundings. The bi-level restaurant includes an outdoor deck that is crowded during the summer months, while inside the restaurant features an open kitchen, which allows guests to peek at the working staff and to enjoy the aromas seeping into the dining area. Cucina Tamar pays great attention to detail, both in terms of its design and its menu. The space includes delicate touches, such as vintage Italian cookbooks, an old-school radio, lovely tablecloths and small vases with fresh flowers. The food, meanwhile, is informed by chef Tamar Cohen-Tzedek's widespread travels across Italy, particularly the Emilia-Romagna region. Cohen-Tzedek has brought home with her secrets from the Italian kitchen, the finest raw ingredients and regional cooking techniques that are highlighted in such dishes as artichoke tortellini, veal scallopini and tagliatelle bandierra—beetroot pasta in a shade of shocking pink, served with mushrooms, asparagus, chard, ricotta and a touch of cream. Cucina Tamar also recently opened a pantry called the Dispensa, where delicacies from the Italian restaurant Amerigo, including its famous balsamic vinegar, are stocked along the shelves of a vintage pharmacy display and are available to the public.

# CHUCHA
43 Sheinkin St.
Tel. (03) 629 1841
*Map/Carte 12*

Chucha is a preferred destination for local fashion mavens who favor distinctive designer clothes with a healthy dose of style and a touch of sex appeal. Each season, Chucha carefully edits its collection of high-quality pieces from Israeli and international brands, pairing it with equally unique accessories, including shoes, handbags and jewelry. The sleek store, which features a concrete floor and exposed white-brick wall, could rival any upscale boutique in New York, Berlin or Paris. Its elegant displays always stock fresh, modern pieces in a multicolored palette that are appropriate for day and night: Whether you prefer funky jeans and a form-flattering leather jacket or feminine blouses and colorful cocktails dresses, you'll find them all at this gem of a boutique.

# RETRO-TLV

123 Yehuda Halevi St.
Tel. (03) 685 0663
www.retro-tlv.com
*Map/Carte* 13

Retro-TLV's centrally located Tel Aviv showroom is a vintage design enthusiast's dream: The shop stocks magnificently restored Israeli and European collectible furniture from the 1950s, '60s and '70s, as well as lighting fixtures and other accessories. Sought-after mid-century modern pieces, including iconic Eames designs and Danish wood furniture, are displayed alongside unique Israeli vintage items, old-school rotary telephones and other hard-to-find period housewares. Retro-TLV firmly believes that vintage design can enhance modern interiors, and the store offers customized consulting to help clients add a touch of the classic to their contemporary homes.

---

## GASTRO PUB
58 Yehuda Halevi St. • Tel. (03) 685 3499

Taking its cue from the traditional London gastro pub, this vibrant restaurant livened up a corner space that had seen a lot of turnover in the past, infusing it with a young clientele that enjoys its hearty pub grub, booze and great music.

## SOCIAL CLUB
45 Rothschild Blvd. • Tel. (03) 560 1114

Located in an intimate piazza in the heart of Tel Aviv, this New York–style bistro offers a diverse menu and inventive cocktails in an aptly social atmosphere.

## ARMADILLO
51 Ahad Ha'am St. • Tel. (03) 620 5573

This unpretentious, incredibly popular neighborhood bar is favored for its friendly vibe, nice selection of beers on tap and simple but delicious Levantine comfort food.

---

## GILDA
64 Ahad Ha'am St. • Tel. (03) 560 3588

Gilda is a stylish and intimate neighborhood bar with knowledgeable bartenders and a quintessentially Tel Aviv vibe.

## DELICATESSEN
5 Barzilay St. • Tel. (03) 560 2297

This bold white-and-yellow boutique showcases the quirky yet sophisticated designs of owner Irit Barak, along with fashion and accessories from other local talents.

## VILLA MAROC
110 Yehuda Halevi St. • Tel. (03) 562 0401

As it name suggests, this colorful shop is dedicated to the best of contemporary Moroccan design, and offers everything from tea sets and textiles to tagines and mosaic-topped tables.

---

## ZIZI TRIPO
7 Carlebach St. • Tel. (03) 561 1597

This spacious underground bar-nightclub hosts renowned electronic DJs, gay-friendly parties and over-the-top events that are generally crowded and ear-shatteringly loud.

## ZINGER
49 Mazeh St. • Tel. (03) 686 8897

Consistently rated one of the best neighborhood bars in Tel Aviv, Zinger recently transformed into more of a lounge bar, but maintained its trademarks: great music and laid-back vibe.

## YAVNE MONTEFIORE
31 Montefiore St. • Tel. (03) 566 6189

The newest addition to star Chef Yonatan Roshfeld's culinary empire, Yavne Montefiore is his take on the classic French bistro, infused with some American touches.

# LEVONTIN 7
7 Levontin St.
Tel. (03) 560 5084
www.levontin7.com
*Map/Carte* 14

Named after its address and located opposite the park in the Gan Hahashmal area, Levontin 7 is both a cozy neighborhood bar-café and one of the most popular live music venues in Israel. The bi-level space consists of a bar-café on the top floor that serves homemade meals during afternoon hours, while at night the space fills up with friends hanging out over drinks as eclectic music plays in the background. Beneath the bar is the performance space, where two live acts take the stage daily. Levontin 7 hosts some of the country's leading bands and musicians, and the performances extend across almost all musical genres: There's alternative rock from top local acts such as Electra, Rona Keinan and others, as well as jazz, classical, electronic and even klezmer offerings. Levontin 7 also hosts music festivals and other events that have a social, political or cultural bent.

*Restaurant • Restaurant*

## TAPAS AHAD HA'AM
27 Ahad Ha'am St. • Tel. (03) 566 6966

This enormously popular tapas restaurant is the creation of Chef Yonatan Roshfeld, recently named a "rising-star chef" by *Food & Wine* magazine. Tapas Ahad Ha'am places great emphasis on the Spanish-style atmosphere, using classic tiles and displays of hanging sausages, while the food combines the finest and freshest Spanish and Israeli ingredients.

*Night • Nuit*

## HAMARKID
30 Ibn Gvirol St.

A new addition to the mega-bar scene, Hamarkid is the latest hot spot for young and beautiful locals and tourists who want to drink and dance until dawn.

*Restaurant • Restaurant*

## YAKIMONO
19 Rothschild Blvd. • Tel. (03) 517 5171/2

Known for its incredibly fresh fish and high-caliber sushi chefs, Yakimono is widely considered the best Japanese restaurant in Israel. Fun fact: It is housed in the building that served as the first U.S. embassy in Israel.

*Fashion • Mode*

## KISIM
8 Hahashmal St. • Tel. (03) 560 4890

Designer Yael Rosen creates handbags and wallets combining clean, elegant design and traditional leather craftsmanship. Her origami-like wallet and coin purse are perfect for an evening out.

*Restaurant • Restaurant*

## CANTINA
71 Rothschild Blvd. • Tel. (03) 620 5051

This lively restaurant overlooking Rothschild Boulevard serves solid Italian fare, and doubles as a great spot for people watching (and, if you're lucky, celeb-spotting).

*Night • Nuit*

## RADIO ROSCO
97 Allenby St. • Tel. (03) 560 0334

Located in a spacious, renovated and hidden courtyard just off noisy Allenby, Radio Rosco serves rustic Italian dishes that are simple and delicious. Their thin-crust pizza continuously gets rave reviews.

*Books • Livres*

## LOTUS
101 Allenby St. • Tel. (03) 566 3630

This old-fashioned, independent bookshop stocks mostly Hebrew titles—ranging from fiction and poetry to philosophy and criticism—usually at a discount.

*Night • Nuit*

## HAPROZDOR
1 Herzl St.

Taking its name from the word "corridor" in Hebrew, this bar is, aptly, entered through a corridor or passageway, which leads to the funky interior of the two-room space. Haprozdor is another favorite among young, hip locals outfitted in second-hand clothing and adorned with mustaches and chunky eyeglasses, who look like transplants from Brooklyn or Berlin.

*Night • Nuit*

## LUCIFER
97 Allenby St. • Tel. (03) 685 1666

This stylish, dimly lit bar is located in a courtyard tucked away off Allenby, and is filled with pictures of saints and other relic-like furniture and décor. Claustrophobics: beware: The place is windowless.

# RUGINE

46 Montefiore St.
Tel. (03) 560 9001
www.rugine.co.il
Map/Carte 15

Located in a beautifully restored building opposite the picturesque Pagoda House in the heart of Tel Aviv, the design house Rugine is a work of art in its own right. Established in 2007 by designer Regin Ganzi, the three-story concept boutique contains 30 rooms showcasing thousands of upscale design pieces. Ganzi planned each of the rooms using a combination of her rich design knowledge and delicate touch, and each one is an enchanting world that tells a unique story. The remarkable space features a diverse array of items that are both manufactured locally and imported from high-end design firms abroad. Among the items Rugine stocks are furniture from the world's leading designers, luxury fabrics and textiles, exceptional accessories, tableware and lighting fixtures and a selection of contemporary Israeli art—anything and everything to outfit your home in the most tasteful and elegant manner.

# RONI KANTOR
64 Rothschild Blvd., 1st floor
Tel. (074) 703 3488
www.ronikantor.co.il
*Map/Carte 16*

Three years ago, when Roni Kantor stumbled upon a trove of vintage dresses she also, in a way, stumbled upon her calling: to work with vintage clothing, crafting individual pieces into something modern with a classic twist. When Kantor's collections outgrew her own apartment, she found them a charming new home. Her recently opened studio, housed in a 1930s villa along Rothschild Boulevard, is a colorful, welcoming space where you feel like a guest or a friend, not a customer. The studio is filled with romantic and flirty dresses, tops and bottoms, each lovingly redesigned, along with vintage-inspired shoes and accessories.

*Café • Café*

## SWING CAFÉ
142 Rothschild Blvd. • Tel. (03) 560 0874

This pleasant and popular café-restaurant sits at the northern end of Rothschild and makes a lovely starting or end point for a leisurely stroll along the boulevard.

*Restaurant • Restaurant*

## FRANK'S
11 Herzl St.

This hot dog/sausage stand is the ultimate late-night stop for those with a bad case of the munchies or those who think something greasy will help prevent their oncoming hangover. Diners can enjoy a variety of hot dogs and sausages with different toppings and sauerkraut in a traditional bun.

*Café • Café*

## SIACH CAFÉ
50 Sheinkin St. • Tel. (03) 528 6352

One of the most veteran cafés on Sheinkin, Siach is situated just opposite the popular garden on the street, making it a pleasant spot to linger over a coffee and watch the colorful goings-on as they happen.

*Café • Café*

## MAZZARINE
42 Montefiore St. • Tel. (03) 566 7020

This elegant café-patisserie truly feels like a small slice of France in Tel Aviv. Located in a beautiful building within the heart of the White City, Mazzarine serves sandwiches, salads and main courses, along with pastries and desserts that are decadent and delicious.

*Café • Café*

## ROTHSCHILD'S
Rothschild Blvd. (at the corner of Mazeh St.)

This famous coffee kiosk along the boulevard is packed with locals around the clock. Pass by on Fridays, when you get to experience the lazy Tel Aviv weekend vibe.

*Night • Nuit*

## CORDUROY
99 Allenby St.

From the owners of the now defunct Rif Raf, one of the most beloved bars among Tel Aviv hipsters, comes Corduroy, another neighborhood bar with a focus on indie-alternative music and outlandish style. You can even feel the irony in the air.

*Night • Nuit*

## TAXIDERMY
18 Harakevet St.

One of the more popular bars in Tel Aviv, Taxidermy has a cool vibe and even cooler clientele—and, yes, stuffed animals constitute a large part of the décor.

*Café • Café*

## BAKERY 29
29 Ahad Ha'am St. • Tel. (03) 560 2020

Do-gooders, take note, this is the place for you: Bakery 29 was founded by a woman who ditched her career on Wall Street and turned to bread and pastries as a way to help others. The menu features sweet and savory pastries, sandwiches and salads, and all proceeds go to a foundation that helps discharged soldiers get educational scholarships.

*Restaurant • Restaurant*

## MEZZE
51a Ahad Ha'am St. • Tel. (03) 629 9753

A favorite among vegetarians, Mezze serves delicious salads, soups and stews, along with Levantine-influenced cuisine and nourishing breakfasts.

# ROTHSCHILD 12

12 Rothschild Blvd.
Tel. (03) 510 6430
www.rothschild12.com
*Map/Carte* **17**

Since making its debut in late 2009, Rothschild 12 has easily become one of the city's hippest hangouts, attracting a cool, sleek, quintessentially Tel Aviv clientele both day and night. The café-bar is located along the historic southern stretch of Rothschild Boulevard in an unassuming building that, despite its slightly rundown appearance, exudes a great amount of charm. The shabby-chic café spills out onto an outdoor patio, where stylish locals sip expertly made coffee and snack on pastries, enjoy comfort food or relax over a hearty brunch on weekends. The structure's industrial appearance also belies what awaits visitors inside: an elegant, incredibly well-stocked bar that serves upscale bistro fare and prides itself on its artistic bent, as evidenced by the grand piano on display. Rothschild 12 hosts renowned DJs and live performances by top musicians practically every evening, and also presents music festivals, contemporary art exhibitions and installations.

## COFFEE BAR

**13 Yad Harutzim St.**
Tel. **(03) 688 9696**
www.coffeebar.co.il
*Map/Carte 18*

Don't be fooled by the name: Coffee Bar is actually a lively restaurant that opened its doors nearly two decades ago in the industrial, somewhat gritty Yad Harutzim neighborhood, and paved the way for other establishments to do the same. Despite its location off the beaten track, Coffee Bar has cemented its reputation as a Tel Aviv institution. It manages to draw crowds day after day, night after night—a testament to its winning formula of classy décor and dynamic atmosphere, excellently prepared food and efficient, friendly service. During lunchtime, Coffee Bar is generally abuzz with the local business and advertising crowd, which comes to take advantage of the generous specials, and that energy generally spills over into the evenings. The menu features Italian-influenced fare and upscale comfort food, including Coffee Bar's famous hamburger in red wine sauce, sautéed chicken livers over mashed potatoes and duck confit, along with daily specials that are listed in chalk on an oversized blackboard. On Fridays, the place fills up with Tel Avivians enjoying the hearty brunch menu, while Saturday lunches at Coffee Bar have developed into a legendary affair. Multiple generations of families sit around large tables and are greeted with antipasti on the house, before indulging in a feast of classic Italian dishes.

**Yaakov Agam's Kinetic Fountain**, 1986, Tzina Dizengoff Sq.

The Center • Le Centre

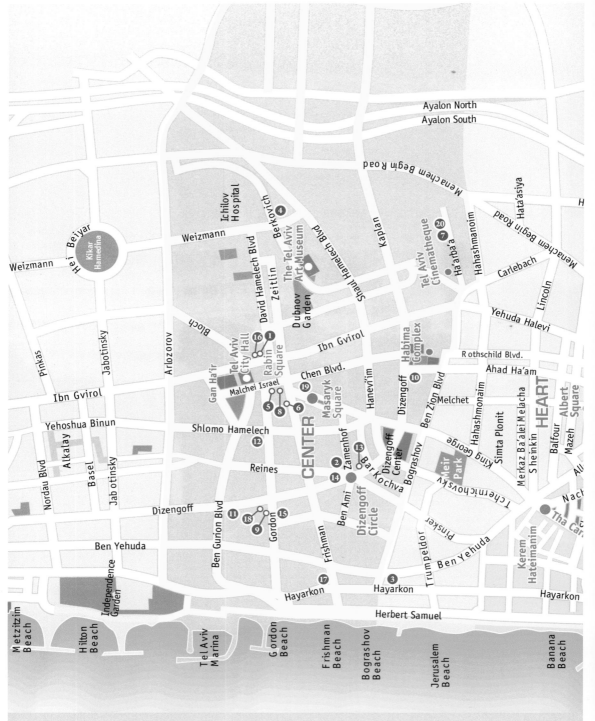

Ayalon North
Ayalon South

Menachem Begin Road

Hatasiya

Hataasiya

Menachem Begin Road

Ichilov Hospital

Berkovich ④

Weizmann

Kikar Hamedina

Hei Beiyar

Weizmann

Zeitlin

David Hamelech Blvd

The Tel Aviv Art Museum

Sderot Hameelech Blvd

Kaplan

Tel Aviv Cinematheque

⑳
⑦
Ha'arba'a

Hahashmanoim

Carlebach

Lincoln

Yehuda Halevi

Pinkas

Jabotinsky

Bloch

Arlozorov

Dubnov Garden

Ibn Gvirol

Habima Complex

Rothschild Blvd.

Ahad Ha'am

Ibn Gvirol

⑯ ①
Tel Aviv City Hall
Gan Ha'ir

Rabin Square

Chen Blvd.
⑲
Masaryk Square

Hanevi'im

Dizengoff
⑩
Ben Zion Blvd
Melchet

Hahashmonaim

HEART

Yehoshua Binun

Malchei Israel
⑤ ⑧ ⑥

Shlomo Hamelech
⑫

Reines

CENTER

Zamenhof
⑬
Bar Kochva

Dizengoff Center

Bograshov

King George

Simta Plonit

Merkaz Ba'alei Melacha

Sheinkin

Balfour

Albert Square

Mazeh

Nordau Blvd

Alkalay

Basel

Jabotinsky

Dizengoff

② 
Ben Ami
⑭

Meir Park

Tchernichovsky

Nach

Ben Gurion Blvd

⑪ ⑮
⑱
⑨
Gordon

Dizengoff Circle

Pinsker

Ben Yehuda

Kerem Hateimanim

Tha Car

Ben Yehuda

Frishman

Trumpeldor

Independence Garden

⑰
Hayarkon

③
Hayarkon

Hayarkon

Herbert Samuel

Metzitzim Beach

Hilton Beach

Tel Aviv Marina

Gordon Beach

Frishman Beach

Bograshov Beach

Jerusalem Beach

Banana Beach

*The Center • Le Centre*

The center of Tel Aviv is an expansive part of the city that blends the quiet, green character of the north end with the energy and activity found in the heart. Central Tel Aviv is where a large number of the city's major cultural institutions can be found, including two branches of the Tel Aviv Museum of Art, the Cameri Theatre, the New Israeli Opera and the cinematheque. In addition to its rich cultural offerings, the center also features historic sites such as Rabin Square and smaller museums dedicated to other prominent figures, as well as newer landmarks like the Azrieli Center that represent Tel Aviv's modernization.

This area is also the part of Tel Aviv that appears to be developing and changing most rapidly: Several renovation projects have already been completed, including the overhaul of the Gordon swimming pool, a Tel Aviv icon, and the expansion of Ibn Gvirol Street—and a number of other projects, including the renovation of Habima Theatre and the restoration of the former German Templer colony Sarona, are in various stages of progress.

The center area also contains inviting spots like Masaryk Square, which is home to stylish boutiques and pleasant cafés, plus other shopping attractions, popular beaches, such as those at Frishman and Gordon Streets, and Tel Aviv's scenic marina. Merging contemporary and old-fashioned Tel Aviv, the center offers plenty of opportunities to get a feel for the city's simultaneously intense and relaxed pace.

## Dizengoff Street

Dizengoff Street has for decades been one of Tel Aviv's most bustling streets, with locals and tourists alike flocking there to shop, stroll or spend time at one of the many cafés and restaurants. From the 1950s to the mid-1970s central Dizengoff was a flourishing cultural hub, where renowned Israeli authors, poets, artists and journalists would congregate at legendary cafés (which, sadly, no longer exist). During its heyday, central Dizengoff was the most fashionable street in Tel Aviv—the place to see and be seen—and its popularity soared to the extent that Israelis even coined a term ("Lehizdangeff," meaning "to Dizengoff") to describe strolling there and enjoying the shopping and cafés. Dizengoff's status dwindled in the late 1970s and '80s, but it has bounced back and is again a thriving commercial street that offers plenty of activity and color both day and night.

## Dizengoff Square

Dizengoff Square, the elevated pedestrian bridge with the multicolored fountain at its center designed by Israeli artist Yaacov Agam, has long been one of the city's most famous landmarks. The original square, built in the 1930s, was at ground level but the site was reconfigured in the 1970s as a bi-level structure to help alleviate traffic congestion. To this day, Tel Avivians engage in heated debates about Dizengoff Square and whether it should be torn down, restored to its original incarnation or redesigned. Until its fate is decided, the square will likely remain the neglected site it is today, one that is used mainly by teenage skateboarders and buskers who perform near the fountain. On Tuesdays and Fridays, there is a flea market beneath the pedestrian bridge, where you can shop for vintage clothing and accessories as well as assorted housewares and knickknacks.

## Dizengoff Center

Israel's first shopping mall, Dizengoff Center, is located at the busy intersection of Dizengoff and King George Streets. Opened in 1977, the enormous structure that contains approximately 400 stores is divided into two sections connected by a skywalk. The center contains a overwhelming mix of local and international clothing and accessories stores, book and magazine shops, specialty stores for comic-book fans, gadget buffs and stamp collectors, an upscale design store, as well as fitness centers, movie theaters and cafés. The center also hosts an international food festival and fashion bazaar on Fridays, where you can sample various cuisines and shop for one-of-a-kind designs. Dizengoff Center isn't Israel's fanciest mall, nor is it its most navigable, but the no-frills environment and relaxed shopping atmosphere are what make it a local favorite.

## Ben-Gurion Boulevard

Named for Israel's first prime minister, Ben-Gurion Boulevard is a quiet, mostly residential street that is lined with leafy trees and punctuated by coffee kiosks and a juice bar that make a perfect pit stop for a leisurely break. There are some remarkable International-style structures here and the Bauhaus building that Ben-Gurion called home is now a museum showcasing personal items, including his impressive library. The boulevard extends west from Rabin Square all the way to the beach, leading to Kikar Atarim—a drab square originally planned as a modern seashore shopping center that never quite lived up to its potential and is considered one of Tel Aviv's great urban planning failures. Today the square is visited mainly for its view of the beach and the Tel Aviv marina, and for the Israeli folk

dancing sessions that take place on the concrete pavement there Saturday afternoons. Just south of Kikar Atarim is the Gordon swimming pool, which in recent years underwent a controversial renovation and now features a minimalist wooden deck and café, where you can sip a coffee and soak up the sun and the mesmerizing view.

## Habima Complex

Ben Zion Boulevard and Chen Boulevard—two pleasant streets for a quiet stroll or bicycle ride—both intersect with the complex housing Habima, Israel's national theater, as well as the Tel Aviv Museum of Art's Helena Rubenstein Pavilion and the Mann Auditorium, home of Israel's philharmonic orchestra. Over the last few years, the theater has undergone a massive, multimillion-dollar facelift—complete with a new façade that literally sparkles. Planned by architect Ram Karmi, the renovation aims to create hundreds of meters of additional space and new state-of-the-art auditoriums. The adjacent square connecting Habima and the Mann Auditorium has also been renovated into a sleek and modern public space designed by renowned Israeli sculptor Dani Karavan.

## Ibn Gvirol Street
## Gan Ha'ir
## Rabin Square
## Masaryk Square

Over the past four years, the municipality has invested millions to expand and renovate Ibn Gvirol, one of the city center's busiest streets, which stretches from Marmorek in the south to the Yarkon River in the north. While the street is decorated with dozens of palm trees and looks shiny and new, the stores and restaurants that line it are an odd assortment: fancy chocolate boutiques and lively restaurants sit alongside old-fashioned falafel shops and orthopedic shoe stores. Ibn Gvirol is also the site of some well-known Tel Aviv landmarks, including City Hall—the imposing rectangular building that contains the city's archives and is known for its faded blue and purple window curtains. Just north of City Hall is Gan Ha'ir, once considered one of Tel Aviv's more elite shopping centers. The two-story mall is arranged around an open courtyard and its upscale clothing and design stores draw a more mature crowd. Gan Ha'ir's roof level houses a cultural center offering lectures, concerts and theatrical productions. To the south of City Hall is Rabin Square, originally called Kings of Israel Square, which was renamed after the assassination of former Prime Minister Yitzhak Rabin at a 1995 peace rally held at the site. There is a monument honoring Rabin beside City Hall, and a portion of the graffiti sprayed on the night of the former leader's murder has also been preserved. Rabin Square is generally a bit desolate, but Israelis still hold peace

rallies and other protests there, along with live music events and an annual book fair. A few minutes' walk from Rabin Square is another square named for Tomas Masaryk, the first president of Czechoslovakia who visited Tel Aviv in the 1920s. Masaryk Square is a charming slice of Tel Aviv life: A number of young fashion designers have opened intimate boutiques there and a couple of excellent cafés overlooking the square, its striking trees and small fountain are lovely spots to linger over lunch or a coffee.

## Shaul Hamelech Boulevard

Named after the biblical figure King Saul, Shaul Hamelech Boulevard may be less regal than other more remarkable thoroughfares in Tel Aviv, but it remains unparalleled in terms of cultural offerings. This is where the main branches of the Tel Aviv Museum of Art and public library are located, as well as the Golda Center, which houses the Cameri Theatre and the Tel Aviv Performing Arts Center, home of the New Israeli Opera. The museum, founded in 1932, possesses an impressive permanent collection of modern and contemporary art and features changing temporary exhibitions; it also houses a cinema and concert hall. The performing arts center presents a varied schedule of classical and jazz concerts and dance performances, while the Cameri—one of Israel's oldest and most venerable theater companies—stages both local and international productions, some with English translation.

## Ha'arba'a Street

Bordered by Carlebach Street and Menachem Begin Road, Ha'arba'a has made a name for itself as one of Tel Aviv's more popular nightlife destinations. The street offers plenty of options for foodies, who can choose from upscale sushi and tapas, pub grub or solid ethnic food from Bulgaria and Turkey, among other cuisines. (Some of the restaurants here also offer excellent deals for lunch.) Culture buffs can catch a film at Tel Aviv's Cinematheque, which is located within the small square just opposite Ha'arba'a Street's western end. The cinema hosts a number of international film festivals throughout the year and screens mainly local and international art-house and indie fare.

## Azrieli Center

This complex of three skyscrapers—one circular, one triangular and one square—symbolizes the new, modern Tel Aviv and is certainly one of the city's most recognizable landmarks. A shopping mall complete with multiplex cinema and food court occupies

Left: **Mandatory Statue #1**. Gabi Klezmer, 1991

**Dudu Geva's Duck**, 2010, Masaryk Sq.

Top: **Holocaust Memorial**, Yigal Tumarkin, 1975. Rabin Sq.

Top: Tel Aviv Marina

the bottom floors of the center, while the towers' main attraction is situated at the top: an observation deck on the 49th floor of the circular building (the second tallest building in Israel), which offers a breathtaking panoramic view of Tel Aviv and beyond.

**Sarona Complex** Located just steps away from the ultra-modern Azrieli Center and surrounded by Defense Ministry and other government offices is another site whose fascinating story adds to Tel Aviv's rich history. It is no coincidence that Sarona—a grassy patch of land dotted with colorful low-rise buildings—resembles a small European village: It was actually a former colony established in 1871 by German Templers who settled in Palestine, bringing with them agricultural and architectural know-how. Since 2003, the municipality has been working to preserve and restore Sarona's unique structures and has even earmarked for protection specific trees planted by the Templers. In the coming years, about 40 of the site's buildings will be transformed into a commercial complex similar to Hatachana near Jaffa, which will house a visitor center and park, along with a mix of boutiques, restaurants and cafés.

# BRASSERIE M&R
70 Ibn Gvirol St.
Tel. **(03) 696 7111**
*Map/Carte **1***

Located in the center of Tel Aviv opposite Rabin Square, this immensely popular French restaurant gives diners the impression they were whisked away to Paris. Every detail of the décor—from the leather banquettes and oversized mirrors to the elongated wooden bar and French/Hebrew menu—is sophisticated but not stuffy. The food, served by attentive waitstaff, is equally refined and meticulously prepared: Excellent starters include Brasserie's famous onion soup and pâté de campagne, while the main courses feature traditional French fare, including steak and moules frites, cassoulet and bœuf bourguignon. Brasserie also serves up one of the juiciest burgers in town (best eaten with their crispy, addictive fries), flavorful poultry and seafood options and creative cocktails from the bar. Open 24 hours a day, Brasserie is one of the only places in Tel Aviv that is hopping both day and night—and despite the clientele that includes an Israeli Who's Who, it still manages to maintain a neighborhood feel.

# CENTER CHIC HOTEL

2 Zamenhof St.
Tel. (03) 526 6100
www.atlas.co.il
*Map/Carte 2*

The culture and spirit of Tel Aviv served as the inspiration for the Center Chic, which is located in Dizengoff Square, at the heart of the city's entertainment area and not far from the beach. Housed in a renewed Bauhaus building, the hotel was fully renovated in early 2011 and contains 54 air-conditioned rooms, most with balconies. The décor features funky furnishings and bold patterns that reflect the city's energy and atmosphere. Amenities include free WiFi throughout the hotel, complimentary bicycle rental, 32-inch televisions and a coffee and tea corner. Guests are invited to relax in the lobby, rooftop lounge or private screening room, where they can enjoy daily complimentary refreshments as well as books or films about Tel Aviv.

# ARTPLUS HOTEL

35 Ben Yehuda St.
Tel. (03) 797 1700
www.atlas.co.il
*Map/Carte 3*

Creative types will surely appreciate this 62-room hotel that is dedicated to Israeli art and is also conveniently located just steps from Tel Aviv's beachfront promenade and the sea. The Artplus commissioned five local artists to create murals that set the decorative tone for each of its floors, and the hotel's foyer and lobby feature works by renowned artists Zadok Ben-David and Sigalit Landau. The cutting-edge rooms feature colorful retro-style furnishings and modern design, which work together to create a comfortable, trendy atmosphere. The hotel also features free WiFi throughout the hotel, complimentary bicycle rental, a cozy outdoor deck, and complimentary refreshments are served in its art-themed library.

# LITVAK GALLERY
4 Berkovich St.
Tel. (03) 695 9496
www.litvakgallery.co.il
*Map/Carte 4*

Litvak Gallery opened in December 2009 and has since firmly established its reputation as one of the city's preeminent art venues. Located in a sleek office tower just steps away from the Tel Aviv Museum of Art, Litvak Gallery presents art exhibitions in various media, but its mission includes the promotion of contemporary glass art to a broad audience. The remarkable space, which covers 800 square meters and features state-of-the-art lighting and technology, provides a sophisticated home for artworks. Since opening, Litvak has hosted several major exhibitions, including a group show featuring 23 of the world's leading glass artists and a breathtaking exhibition of 100 works by the internationally renowned artist Dale Chihuly. The gallery space also extends to a charming balcony, where viewers can glimpse dazzling artworks against the backdrop of the Tel Aviv skyline.

*Chihuly at Litvak, 2011*

# BOOKWORM

9 Malchei Israel St.
Tel. **(03) 529 8490**
www.bookworm.co.il
*Map/Carte* **5**

Tucked away on a quiet strip behind Rabin Square, Bookworm has for years been a favorite among local bibliophiles who appreciate its extensive selection and enjoy its tranquil atmosphere. The bright, inviting shop specializes in the fields of psychology, architecture and design, but also carries fiction and non-fiction titles in Hebrew and English along with a wide array of poetry books, children's books and literary and arts journals. The bookshop also houses a quaint café, where you can enjoy a coffee and cake or order a light meal while paging through one of the titles on display.

---

*Restaurant • Restaurant*

### TOTO
4 Berkovich St. • Tel. (03) 693 5151

Wunderkind Chef Yaron Shalev has transformed this classy spot serving upscale Mediterranean cuisine into one of Tel Aviv's most highly regarded restaurants.

*Night • Nuit*

### SEX BOUTIQUE
122 Dizengoff St. • Tel. (03) 544 4555

Located above a sex shop of the same name, the atmosphere here is far from sleazy—it's actually an elegant neighborhood pick-up bar featuring a soundtrack mainly from the 1960s and '70s.

*Fashion • Mode*

### ANNA K.
75 Frishman St. • Tel. (03) 529 1244

This tiny shop carries quirky, indie-inspired women's clothes and accessories, and has something of a cult following among the city's fashionistas.

---

*Fashion • Mode*

### A+
172 Dizengoff St. • Tel. (03) 527 1728

Featuring color-coordinated collections of sexy tops, flirty dresses and more, A+ has something for every woman at prices that won't break the bank.

*Fashion • Mode*

### KAY
159 Dizengoff St. • Tel. (03) 522 9552

Taking its name from the Japanese word meaning "cute," this lively boutique updates its collection every two months with fresh clothing from Japan, Hong Kong, Korea and Europe.

*Restaurant • Restaurant*

### MOON
58 Bograshov St. • Tel. (03) 629 1155

Located on buzzing Bograshov Street, this fashionable Japanese eatery serves up conveyor belt sushi straight out of downtown Tokyo.

---

*Fashion • Mode*

### RHUS OVATA
155 Dizengoff St. • Tel. (03) 523 3162

Cutting-edge fashion created by sisters Einav and Hadas Zucker, talented young designers whose clothes are coveted by trend-makers, not followers.

*Night • Nuit*

### THE CAT & THE DOG
23 Carlebach St.

A dark, fashionable underground bar-club that oozes sex appeal and regularly hosts some of the finest DJs around. Beware: Lines to get in are long, especially over the weekend.

*Fashion • Mode*

### TAKE A NAP
17 Masaryk Sq. • Tel. (03) 527 1757

Lovely clothes and accessories for moms and their babies: ridiculously soft, high-quality fabrics in a subtle palette of blues, pinks, grays and whites.

# OLIA
73 Frishman St.
Tel. (03) 522 3235
www.olia.co.il
*Map/Carte 6*

Olia is a paean to olive oil. This enchanting boutique draws in passersby with its striking design, and then seduces them with a feast of flavors and scents. The fire-engine-red shelves are lined with hundreds of bottles of extra virgin olive oil from all over Israel, and each variety has a distinctive history and attributes. The boutique offers customers a unique educational and sensory experience by encouraging them to taste and smell the oils before selecting the one that best suits their needs. Olia also offers a broad variety of seasonal gourmet delicacies, including vinaigrettes, tapenades, pickled olives, mustards, spice blends and herbal tea infusions, all of which are locally produced and celebrate the diversity of Middle Eastern customs and cuisines. In addition, the store carries an exclusive line of pampering spa products, made with the finest natural ingredients and—what else?—olive oil.

# MESSA

19 Ha'arba'a St.
Tel. (03) 685 6859
www.messa.co.il
*Map/Carte 7*

Messa fundamentally upgraded the Tel Aviv culinary landscape when it opened six years ago to overwhelming accolades. Since then Chef Aviv Moshe's haute cuisine—which is grounded in Provençal cooking but influenced by his Kurdish roots—has continued to surprise and delight diners. The menu, which changes with the seasons, includes an intriguing blend of tastes and textures, created using only the finest ingredients. Among the unique courses are a caramelized foie gras carpaccio appetizer, served with tahini paste, date honey and black sea salt flakes; a main course of seafood couscous in a crab, lemon and thyme broth; and a coconut cappuccino dessert with baked cheese, lemon cream and frozen pineapple, among other sumptuous sweets. All of these can be enjoyed with a selection from the exceptional wine list or one of Messa's signature cocktails. Apart from the imaginative cuisine, Messa is also known for its stunning interior design by Alex Meitlis. The white-on-white interior—with its cascading white drapes, long marble tables stretching across the restaurant and comfortable, ultramodern seating alcoves—is simply a sight to behold. Guests can also enjoy a pre-dinner drink and sample the menu at the equally dramatic black-on-black bar next door.

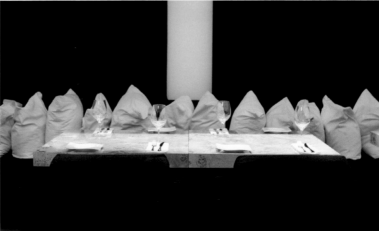

# MAYU
7 Malchei Israel St.
Tel. (03) 527 3992
www.mayu.co.il
*Map/Carte 8*

In 2004, when Maya Zukerman opened this first branch of Mayu, she helped usher in something of a fashion renaissance around Rabin Square and the surrounding area. Mayu has long been a favorite among casually chic Tel Aviv women of all ages, who appreciate the boutique's clean yet elegant designs and high-quality natural and organic fabrics. Most of Mayu's collection is designed in-house, but Zukerman also showcases established and up-and-coming Israeli peers who use locally grown fibers, as well as French, Italian and British designers who share a similar aesthetic. The boutique itself, with its stark white walls, floors and display cases, provides an intimate home for the subdued yet sensuous designs.

---

*Restaurant • Restaurant*

## THAI HOUSE
8 Bograshov St. • Tel. (03) 517 8568

This ever-crowded eatery is simply the best Thai restaurant in Israel. Reservations highly recommended.

*Fashion • Mode*

## THE BRUNCH
17 Gordon St. • Tel. (03) 602 1602

This super-trendy women's clothing boutique imports high-end European brands and caters to a mostly well-to-do and celebrity clientele.

*Concept Store • Magasin spécialisé*

## BAUHAUS CENTER
99 Dizengoff St. • Tel. (03) 522 0249

Devoted to everything Bauhaus in Tel Aviv, this center stocks books, posters and works by local artists; it also hosts changing exhibitions about the White City's history and offers guided tours in Hebrew, English and French of the city's World Heritage sites.

---

*Restaurant • Restaurant*

## TAPEO
16 Ha'arba'a St. • Tel. (03) 624 0484

There's always a festive mood at this Spanish-style tapas bar, where the lighting is dim, the setting is sexy and the bar is always action-packed.

*Night • Nuit*

## AUTO 76
76 Ibn Gvirol St.

From the owners of the Galina mega bar comes this well-designed underground pick-up bar. In addition to the well-stocked bar, there's also a pool table and '80s arcade games.

*Fashion • Mode*

## IMUMA
144 Dizengoff St. • Tel. (077) 443 0632

Imuma is an ode to contemporary Israeli shoe design—it stocks only locally produced, beautifully handmade shoes from some of the hottest homegrown talents.

---

*Restaurant • Restaurant*

## AMORE MIO
100 Ibn Gvirol St. • Tel. (03) 524 4040

This Italian institution serves up delicious home-style food in a warm and welcoming atmosphere that is family-friendly—and even includes a "papa" who greets you at the door.

*Restaurant • Restaurant*

## ONAMI
18 Ha'arba'a St. • Tel. (03) 562 1172

Consistently praised as one of the best sushi spots in the city, Onami's best-kept secret is its excellent three-course lunch special on weekdays.

*Fashion • Mode*

## ANYA FLEET
21 Masaryk Sq. • Tel. (03) 523 7497

Located in the fashionable Masaryk Square area, this chic boutique excels at bridal gowns and eveningwear featuring thoroughly feminine, flowy silhouettes.

# ARBITMAN'S

31 Gordon St.
Tel. (03) 527 8254
www.arbitmans.com
*Map/Carte 9*

Arbitman's design gallery, known locally as "the design pearl of Gordon Street," is one of the freshest, most innovative and beloved design galleries in Israel. The New York-style gallery offers an eclectic mix of pieces that are exclusively imported from leading design capitals around the world. Among the items showcased are some featuring classic and traditional design, and others that are groundbreaking and avant-garde. Arbitman's devotes considerable space to high-quality design made in Israel; in this section, you can find design pieces from collections that were created by the Arbitman's team as well as works by renowned Israeli designers. The gallery also devotes space to a permanent exhibition of original works and digital prints by international Pop Art artist Natan Elkanovich. In recent years, Arbitman's has also begun to market select items to museum stores and boutiques internationally. The personality who leads the store's vision is proprietor Benny Arbitman, a veteran interior designer and award-winning art director in Israel's film and television industry.

# CLAUDE SAMUEL
17 Dizengoff St.
(corner of Tarsat Blvd.)
Tel. (03) 620 8882/3
www.csamuel.co.il
*Map/Carte 10*

You could say optometry is in Claude Samuel's genes: The senior optometrist at Tel Hashomer hospital is descended from a long line of French optometrists that have been practicing since 1848. At his private clinic/boutique—perched on a corner opposite the Habima complex—Samuel offers clients comprehensive eye examinations lasting about half an hour, which are followed by the fun part: selecting the perfect frame from the endless rows of mostly imported, high-quality glasses on display. The dedicated, courteous staff helps customers choose just the right frame to match each individual's style. Fans of retro design are encouraged to seek out Samuel's own line of vintage-inspired eyewear or the authentic vintage frames secretly stashed among the drawers. History buffs will enjoy studying pieces from Samuel's 800-piece private collection of glasses, antique optometry equipment and binoculars for theater and opera.

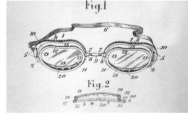

# SARAH BRAUN
162 Dizengoff St.
Tel. (03) 529 9902
*Map/Carte 11*

Since opening her store seven years ago, Sarah Braun has cemented her reputation as one of Israel's finest and freshest designers by consistently creating quirky, minimalist collections that never go out of style. Braun has straddled both French and Israeli culture from a young age, and she applies this multicultural background to her designs, which blend relaxed European-style cuts with high-quality fabrics that are light and comfortable enough to suit the hottest summer day. Braun has long been a favorite among strong, distinctive Israeli women; with her recently launched menswear line, guys can get in on the action as well.

---

*Restaurant • Restaurant*

### GOOCHA
14 Ibn Gvirol St. • Tel. (03) 691 1603

A fish and seafood restaurant favored for its high-quality food with interesting flavor combinations and extremely reasonable prices.

*Beauty • Beauté*

### YULIA MANICURE
101 Dizengoff St. • Tel. (1700) 707 706

One of the trendiest places in the city to get pampered, Yulia offers mani-pedis and more in a vibrant, club-like atmosphere.

*Night • Nuit*

### MOLLY BLOOM'S
2 Mendele St. • Tel. (03) 522 1558

This classic Irish pub is frequented by English-speaking expats, who gather here to watch rugby and football matches on enormous screens accompanied by a few pints of Guinness.

---

*Restaurant • Restaurant*

### MEAT BAR
52 Chen Blvd. • Tel. (03) 695 6276

The name says it all: This intimate space serving up freshly grilled meat is a carnivore's delight.

*Design • Design*

### NOOK
5 Malchei Israel St. • Tel. (03) 527 7177

This stylish shop tucked away behind Rabin Square specializes in eclectic Asian-inspired clothing, accessories and housewares.

*Fashion • Mode*

### IDO RECANATI
13 Malchei Israel St. • Tel. (03) 529 8481

Ido Recanati's casually chic designs blend modern geometric shapes with bold colors and graphic compositions.

---

*Fashion • Mode*

### ANAT MIKULINSKY
127 Dizengoff St. • Tel. (03) 523 5180

Anat Mikulinsky hails from a famous fashion family in Tel Aviv, and her eclectic, reasonably priced boutique offers something for everyone.

*Night • Nuit*

### PEACOCK
14 Marmorek St. • Tel. (03) 686 8259

One of the most popular neighborhood bars in Tel Aviv, Peacock is perpetually crowded with cool Tel Avivians who flock here to enjoy its laid-back vibe and upscale pub grub.

*Fashion • Mode*

### PRECIOUS
63 Frishman St. • Tel. (03) 529 3814

This adorable shop stocks the trendiest footwear brands from Israel and abroad, along with a well-edited selection of vintage-inspired clothing.

# SHAY ARYE GALLERY

61 Shlomo Hamelech St.
(corner of Gordon St.)
Tel. (03) 696 7196
Mobile (052) 831 1664
www.shayaryegallery.com
*Map/Carte* **12**

Shay Arye Gallery is nestled on a corner where quiet, tree-lined Shlomo Hamelech meets Gordon Street—a hub of the traditional Tel Aviv art scene—but this is far from a conventional art space. Since opening in 2008, Shay Arye has been lauded in the Israeli press for its fresh, often experimental presentation of contemporary art. The alternative art venue presents exhibitions that explore various topics and use multiple media, including painting, photography, video art and sculpture. The gallery also fosters dialogue about art by pairing Israeli artists with their European counterparts in their exhibitions and by offering gallery talks for visitors.

## REVIVA AND CELIA
24 Ha'arba'a St. • Tel. (03) 561 8617

Following its success in Ramat Hasharon, Reviva and Celia opened a branch of their patisserie and café in Tel Aviv, bringing with them their incredible array of sweets and baked goods.

## RONEN CHEN
155 Dizengoff St. • Tel. (03) 527 5672

One of the best-known names in local fashion, Ronen Chen has garnered a loyal following for his clean-lined casual separates for women.

## CALA
184 Dizengoff St. • Tel. (03) 529 0260

Offering an extensive and colorful collection of flirty and feminine tops, dresses and accessories, along with a unique vintage collection, Cala is a darling among Tel Aviv's fashion-forward crowd.

## RAPHAEL
87 Hayarkon St. • Tel. (03) 522 6464

Consistently rated one of the best restaurants in Tel Aviv, Raphael is the brainchild of Chef Rafi Cohen, who creates wonderfully modern takes on Mediterranean and Moroccan dishes.

## SHINE
12 Masaryk Sq. • Tel. (03) 529 8607

This tiny boutique carries women's fashion characterized by clean lines, natural fabrics and a neutral color palette.

## SHANI BAR
151 Dizengoff St. • Tel. (03) 527 8451

One of the most talented local shoe designers, Shani Bar is renowned for footwear featuring unique styles and buttery leather.

## MIZNON
21 Ibn Gvirol St. • Tel. (03) 716 8977

A new venture by celebrity Chef Eyal Shani, who is famous for his eccentric, tomato-loving style, this casual joint serves upscale pita sandwiches in a cafeteria-like setting.

## WINE ROUTE – SHAKED BROTHERS
93 Hahashmonaim St. • Tel. (03) 561 9263

One of the best specialty wine shops in Tel Aviv, Wine Route carries an extensive selection; hosts tastings and workshops; and its professional staff offers visitors comprehensive explanations of different vineyards and vintages.

## LEIBLING
63 Bar Kochva St. • Tel. (03) 525 1020

Footwear designers Karni Reshef and Lior Livne create limited editions of beautifully crafted leather shoes with an artistic twist.

# AMELIA
88 Dizengoff St.
Tel. (03) 528 3888
*Map/Carte 13*

Named after aviatrix Amelia Earhart, this fashionable neighborhood café-bistro opened 70 years to the day of her disappearance, and is decorated with photographs of the missing pilot and outlines of her route. Amelia's menu also draws inspiration from the globetrotting heroine: innovative dishes blend flavors from the classic American kitchen with touches from France, Italy and Israel. The café's eclectic dishes include delightful breakfasts, savory tarts and sandwiches, crisp salads, homemade pastas and upscale comfort food like burgers and chicken wings—all made using the freshest ingredients. Amelia is centrally located near Dizengoff Square, so you can people watch while sipping a perfectly prepared coffee.

# CINEMA HOTEL
1 Zamenhof St.
Tel. (03) 520 7100
www.atlas.co.il
*Map/Carte 14*

Housed in a renovated Bauhaus building that was one of the first movie theaters in Tel Aviv, the Cinema offers the intimacy of a boutique hotel in a central location just steps away from shopping and entertainment, and a short walk from the beach. Its décor is clean and modern, but with a retro edge that is reflected in film posters and original movie projectors that serve as design accents. The hotel features a beautiful rooftop terrace, sauna and Jacuzzi, and rooms include free WiFi, complimentary bicycle rental, a hot beverage corner, mini refrigerator and safe. Daily complimentary refreshments are served in the lounge, and classic movies are screened in the lobby and served with complimentary popcorn.

# OBERSON FASHION HOUSE

36 Gordon St.
Tel. (03) 524 3822
www.karenoberson.com
*Map/Carte 15*

For nearly 40 years, the name Gideon Oberson has been synonymous with the crème de la crème of Israeli high fashion. Oberson is renowned for his exquisite swimwear collections, which feature modern shapes, clean lines and quality construction, and have on more than one occasion been referred to as "wearable art." Oberson instills the same creativity and flawless attention to detail in his prêt-à-porter and custom-designed eveningwear lines, which have a devoted following among elegant women in Israel and abroad. Oberson's stylish showroom also carries KO, the line designed by his daughter Karen, which has brought the Oberson name a whole new legion of fans.

*Restaurant • Restaurant*

## ZEPRA

96 Yigal Alon St. • Tel. (03) 624 0044

Called a "stunner" by *Wallpaper* magazine, Chef Avi Conforti's sleek Asian-fusion eatery is also a great spot for late-night drinks if you happen to be in the neighborhood.

*Night • Nuit*

## HAMARA

87 Hayarkon St. • Tel. (03) 522 6464

Hamara is the swanky bar within the restaurant Raphael, where you can enjoy inventive after-dinner cocktails such as fig, apricot or spicy martinis, or sample smaller offerings from the menu.

*Restaurant • Restaurant*

## MERCADO

Azrieli Center • Tel. (03) 609 3030

Taking its name from the word for "market" in Spanish, this kosher restaurant from Chef Avi Biton of Adora fame offers an eclectic menu against the backdrop of sweeping views of Tel Aviv.

*Concept Store • Magasin spécialisé*

## THE THIRD EAR

48 King George St. • Tel. (03) 621 5200

The best music shop and DVD library in Tel Aviv, the Third Ear is known for its young staff of incredibly knowledgeable music geeks and film buffs.

*Café • Café*

## MASARYK CAFE

12 Masaryk Sq. • Tel. (03) 527 2411

Overlooking the charming Masaryk Square, this cozy café is a great place to linger over a coffee and croissant or enjoy a big, healthy salad.

*Night • Nuit*

## SILON

129 Ibn Gvirol St. • Tel. (03) 546 4096

One of the most popular neighborhood bars in Tel Aviv, Silon is known for its well-stocked bar, good music and friendly service.

*Concept Store • Magasin spécialisé*

## WINE & MORE – HINNAWI

25 Carlebach St. • Tel. (03) 624 0458

A specialty gourmet shop selling a wide selection of wine and wine accessories, along with delicacies including high-end meats and cheeses.

*Fashion • Mode*

## SALON SALOME

25 Gordon St. • Tel. (03) 527 4150

Owned by friends Meital Levy and Della Berger, Salon Salome offers clothes and jewelry created by Israeli designers, alongside vintage Israeli pottery, furniture and other flea market finds.

*Night • Nuit*

## ARMADILLO CERVEZA

174 Dizengoff St. • Tel. (03) 529 3277

The sister of the original Armadillo on Ahad Ha'am Street, Armadillo Cerveza brings the winning mix of hip clientele, wide assortment of beer on tap and superb Middle Eastern bar food to the city center. Grab a seat early—it tends to get packed.

# BAKERY

72 Ibn Gvirol St.
Tel. (03) 696 1050
www.bakerytlv.co.il
*Map/Carte 16*

Residents of central Tel Aviv breathed a collective sigh of relief when this second branch of Bakery opened on Ibn Gvirol, as they would no longer have to trek to Yad Harutzim to get a fix of their favorite baked goods. When it comes to Bakery, though, the term "baked goods" is an understatement: The buttery croissants, moist muffins, beautifully arranged fruit tarts and tartes tatins, creamy éclairs and freshly baked breads and cakes are worthy of their own category—something along the lines of "baked bests." This tiny gem of a place is regularly packed with patrons who bring their newspapers or laptops, pull up a seat at one of the marble-topped tables and spend several minutes deciding in which pastry to indulge. On Friday mornings, customers line up early as the goods literally sell like hotcakes.

# PRIMA TEL AVIV

105 Hayarkon St.
Tel. (03) 520 6666
www.prima.co.il
*Map/Carte* **17**

The Prima Tel Aviv hotel blends the vitality and culture of the White City with the comfort and intimacy of home. Located just steps away from Tel Aviv's breathtaking beachfront and within walking distance from other attractions, the Prima offers discerning travelers a combination of professional service and central location. The décor of each of the hotel's floors is inspired by Israeli cultural figures who lived and worked in Tel Aviv, and the 60 air-conditioned rooms, including 20 deluxe rooms, mostly face the Mediterranean. Amenities include complimentary in-room hot beverage corner, flat-screen television, mini refrigerator and safe; free WiFi is available in the hotel, for an additional fee. Guests can also get a dose of culture at the in-house Prima Gallery, which exhibits contemporary Israeli artists.

Concept Store • Magasin spécialisé

# LE PALAIS DES THÉS

131 Dizengoff St.
Tel. (03) 522 1317
www.palaisdesthes.co.il
*Map/Carte 18*

Since opening its first store in Israel in 2010, the Palais des Thés has transformed countless Tel Avivians into tea enthusiasts—which is no small feat considering locals' diehard devotion to coffee. The 25-year-old company's aim is to make tea accessible by taking customers on a virtual journey to discover the cultures of tea, and introduce them to the countless varieties, their aromas and flavors. This elegant boutique, decorated with colorful photographs of tea plantations, carries more than 200 varieties of the best white, green, oolong, black and red teas from China, Taiwan, Japan, India, Sri Lanka, South Africa and other exotic countries. Loose teas are stored in rows of aluminum tins and are sold by weight, or come pre-packaged in colorful metal canisters or in packs of tea bags. Le Palais des Thés also carries a range of beautiful accessories, including teapots and cups, which make wonderful gifts on a special occasion—or even on a regular day.

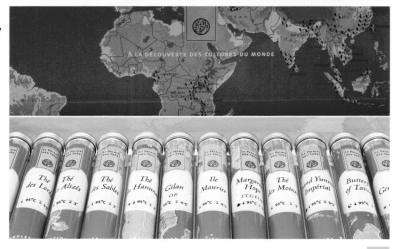

# LIBRAIRIE DU FOYER

14 Masaryk Sq.
Tel. (03) 524 3835
www.librairie.co.il
*Map/Carte* **19**

Librairie du Foyer is the perfect embodiment of a neighborhood bookstore: It is quaint and welcoming, with worn-in wood floors and mosaic decorations and, most important, shelves upon shelves of fiction and non-fiction titles, along with cookbooks, children's books and titles translated from French to Hebrew and vice versa. The shop has catered to Tel Aviv's French speakers since 1968, and has grown to be Israel's largest French bookstore under current proprietor Myriam Ezra. Librairie du Foyer also serves as a community center, offering lectures with French authors and philosophers, as well as a weekly story hour for kids.

## LILUSH
73 Frishman St. • Tel. (03) 537 9354

This charming neighborhood café serves up tasty panini sandwiches, hearty pasta dishes and other healthy fare. It's also one of the only places in Tel Aviv to serve soup year-round.

## YANGA
69 Dizengoff St. • Tel. (03) 620 1115

Yanga offers trendy, feminine and contemporary women's wear and accessories at exceptionally reasonable prices.

## DIZENGOFF
16 Ben Ami St.

Centrally located adjacent to Dizengoff Square, this new mega bar features three bars, a dance floor, cozy couches and a VIP room for special events. The owners are several well-known Tel Aviv actors, so you never know whom you might spot there.

## BACCIO
85 King George St. • Tel. (03) 528 9753

Baccio is a favorite among hipsters, intellectuals and film-school types who come to hang out, work on their laptops or just linger over a coffee while reading the paper. Baccio offers light café fare and also has a nice selection of homemade ice creams.

## HANUT BGADIM
78 Dizengoff St. • Tel. (03) 529 3277

A small flight of stairs leads to Hanut Bgadim, meaning "clothing store" in Hebrew. The charming boutique stocks local designers' creations alongside imported items, jeans, jewelry and accessories and a private collection of vintage designs.

## THE STREETS
2 Hanevi'im St. • Tel. (03) 620 1070

This pleasant café is located along busy King George Street, but offers a quiet respite from the hustle and bustle. The food is excellent and the service is friendly, and it's also open 24 hours.

## WINE BAR BOUTIQUE
83 King George St. • Tel. (03) 525 9911

This neighborhood bar caters to wine enthusiasts who want to try something new when they go out: It offers 90 vintages with a changing selection of wines by the glass, and charges patrons by the centimeter, with glasses ranging from NIS 29-49. It also offers a small menu of appetizers, salads and focaccia.

## SHINE
38 Shlomo Hamelech St. • Tel. (03) 527 6186

Shine is one of those neighborhood cafés that is perennially packed: During the day, patrons come to enjoy the filling breakfasts and crisp salads, while at night the ambience is more bar-like. Its sleek white interior has a retro feel, and the magazine rack always stocks the latest indie fashion and design publications.

# MOADON HAKTZINIM

21 Ha'arba'a St.
Tel. (03) 685 1154
www.giraffe.co.il
*Map/Carte 20*

# GIRAFFE NOODLE BAR

49 Ibn Gvirol St.
Tel. (03) 691 6294
www.giraffe.co.il
*Map/Carte 21*

Israel's culinary landscape changed in 1996 with the opening of Giraffe, the first pan-Asian restaurant to pair dishes inspired by far-flung countries such as China, Japan, Thailand, Malaysia and the Philippines with classic European desserts. The recently redesigned restaurant is stylish but casual, and offers pleasant sidewalk seating. There are a number of outstanding starters, including a flavorful tofu salad and piquant Thai soup. Giraffe's wonderfully seasoned main courses—including excellent spicy noodle dishes and the refreshing crispy beef dish—have the power to draw customers back again and again. On the heels of Giraffe's success, its owners opened the more upscale Moadon Haktzinim ("Officers' Club") four years ago. The sleek space is a modern take on British and French colonial dining halls, and features an eclectic menu combining Giraffe's all-time favorites with more elaborate dishes and an exceptional wine list.

*The North • Le Nord*

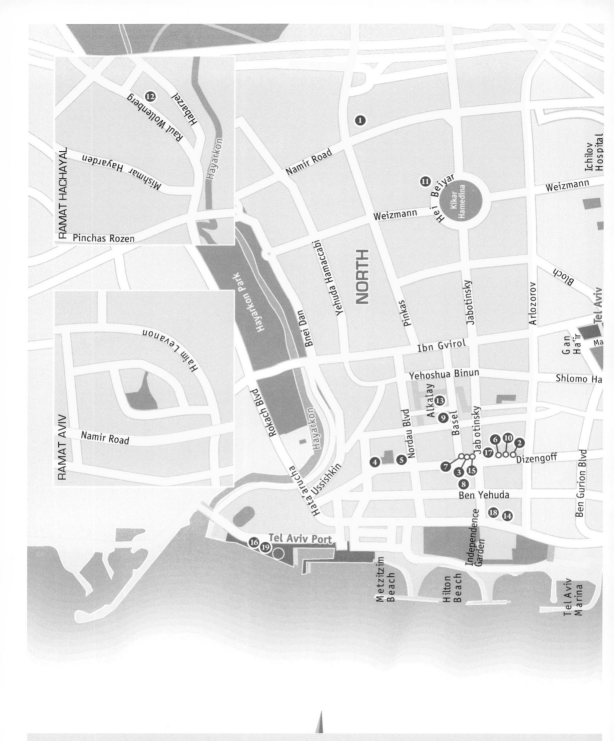

RAMAT HACHAYAL

Raul Wollenberg

Habatzel

Hayarkon

Mishmar Hayarden

Pinchas Rozen

RAMAT AVIV

Halm Levanon

Namir Road

Namir Road

Hayarkon Park

Bnei Dan

Yehuda Hamaccabi

Weizmann

Hei Beivar

Kikar Hamedina

Weizmann

Bloch

Ichilov Hospital

NORTH

Pinkas

Jabotinsky

Arlozorov

Tel Aviv

Gan Ha'ir

Ma

Ibn Gvirol

Yehoshua Binun

Shlomo Ha

Rokach Blvd

Hayarkon

Hata'arucha

Ha'ta Ussishkin

Nordau Blvd

Alkalay

Basel

Jabotinsky

Dizengoff

Ben Gurion Blvd

Ben Yehuda

Independence Garden

Metzitzim Beach

Hilton Beach

Tel Aviv Marina

Tel Aviv Port

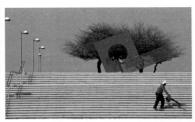

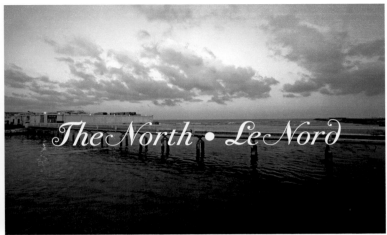

# The North • Le Nord

The north end of Tel Aviv feels more like a sleepy suburb compared with other parts of the city: It's less crowded than the south, less bustling than the heart of Tel Aviv or its center, and many of its streets are quiet and tree-lined, especially around Hayarkon Park, Tel Aviv University and the various neighborhoods that make up Ramat Aviv. Parts of the north end exude a feeling of old-time Tel Aviv. This is where you're more likely to notice the smell of grandma's chicken soup or schnitzel wafting in the air on Friday afternoons as the city begins to wind down for the weekend. And despite the recent renovation of Ibn Gvirol Street, one of the area's main thoroughfares, it remains lined with mom-and-pop shops whose fading signs advertise everything from books and clothing to pastries and falafel.

The north end of Tel Aviv is also greener than neighboring parts of the city thanks in part to Hayarkon Park, the sprawling green sanctuary that is the perfect backdrop for a relaxed bike ride or quiet walk along one of its paths, or for a family picnic, which has become something of a tradition on Saturdays as locals flock there for some weekend downtime. The north also contains a greater concentration of small parks and playgrounds, which cater to young urban professionals and their families and to aging residents, who can often be seen sitting on benches and chatting in groups with their mostly foreign caretakers.

This section of Tel Aviv is often considered more homogeneous than neighborhoods further south and traditionally has been viewed as the European-influenced (read: Ashkenazi) and bourgeois part of town. In fact, over the years, the area has come to be associated with wealth to such a degree that Israelis even have a nickname for north Tel Aviv residents: "tsfonim" (literally "northerners" in Hebrew), a slang and somewhat derogatory term that implies affluence and what some perceive as a certain accompanying snobbishness.

North Tel Aviv is certainly where well-to-do locals and visitors alike make good use of their credit cards at high-end boutiques along Dizengoff Street, at the fashionable Ramat Aviv shopping mall or in Kikar Hamedina ("the State's Square"), the circular

square that is home to stores offering dozens of international luxury brands and upscale Israeli designers. In recent years, the north end has also seen multiple multimillion-dollar residential housing projects—including one developed with international design star Philippe Starck—crop up, forever altering their surroundings and the city's skyline.

Despite these lucrative projects, the north is actually less renowned for its architecture than other parts of the White City. Tel Aviv's wealth of International style buildings that have grown to be the city's hallmark never quite made it to this part of town, which features boxier, unremarkable residential buildings.

Regardless, the area known for its laid-back atmosphere still has plenty of draws: the renovated port, several worthwhile museums and some of Tel Aviv's best and most popular beaches, including Hilton Beach (commonly referred to as the gay or gay-friendly beach) and Hof Metzitzim ("Peeping Tom's Beach" in Hebrew), which was immortalized in a 1970s cult film.

## North Dizengoff

Dizengoff Street, once the focal point of Israeli bohemia, has long been synonymous with shopping, strolling and enjoying leisurely get-togethers at cafés. The stretch of north Dizengoff Street has for years been a prime destination for Tel Avivians in search of the latest fashions, and today the strip is jam-packed with stores carrying everything from casual, vintage-inspired clothes and handmade leather shoes to elegant wedding gowns and well-tailored suits. Nearly all of Israel's top designers have a boutique along Dizengoff Street and many up-and-coming local talents aspire to join their ranks one day.

North Dizengoff is also home to a surprising number of bridal boutiques and, while visiting the area, it's not uncommon to see brides-to-be getting fitted for their big day or even emerging onto the street in ornate gowns, with perfect hair and make-up, just a short time ahead of the ceremony.

Yarkon River

**Basel Square**  Not far from Dizengoff Street is Basel Square, a charming piazza-like area that houses a nice mix of restaurants, cafés and bakeries, gourmet and specialty food shops, designer housewares stores and a top-notch local bookstore that carries a large selection of English books, journals and magazines. In recent years, a handful of upscale designer boutiques that can rival any on Dizengoff Street have also opened their doors around the square.

**Kikar Hamedina**  Kikar Hamedina, Tel Aviv's posh circular "square" has for decades been where the city's upper crust goes to get (or where the less well-off go to look at) the latest trends off runways in Paris and London. The square dates back to before the establishment of the state, with some of the land having been purchased in 1942, while the low-rise residential buildings surrounding the grassy field at its center were erected in the 1970s. All the top international luxury brands can be found here: Armani, Balenciaga, Gaultier, Gucci, Prada, Yves Saint Laurent, Louis Vuitton and Burberry.

**Tel Aviv Port**  Founded in 1936, the Tel Aviv Port was the first Hebrew docking port established in Mandate Palestine, and today it is considered one of the foremost examples of successful urban renewal in Israel: What was once a decaying and neglected eyesore is now a thriving center of activity owing to a substantial renovation that got underway in 2001. The restoration project aimed to blend modern elements with historical remains, and it left some of the decades-old shipping apparatus intact while constructing a vivacious entertainment center in the surrounding area. The renovation earned Udi Kassif and Ganit Maislits Kassif, the two architects who designed its public spaces, the award for outstanding landscape architecture at the 2010 European Biennial for Landscape Architecture, in Barcelona. The port's spectacular waterfront has a 20,000-square-meter wooden boardwalk lined with restaurants, trendy bars and nightclubs where visitors can eat and drink while enjoying a view of the Mediterranean. The port also hosts exhibitions and concerts in its hangars, and is also home to a thriving farmer's market, a spa and numerous clothing stores. This is one part of Tel Aviv that hardly ever comes to a standstill, as exercise fanatics take advantage of it for jogging, roller-blading or outdoor yoga and spinning classes, while families come out in droves on Saturday afternoons and night-owls hit the clubs and mega bars after dark.

**Yehuda Hamaccabi**

Yehuda Hamaccabi Street extends from Ibn Gvirol to the residential Bavli neighborhood further east, and it provides a relaxing spot for a quiet getaway within the city. Yehuda Hamaccabi and the surrounding streets are considered some of the hottest real estate in Tel Aviv, as the area comprises a mix of low-rise apartment buildings and private villas with well-kept gardens. Yehuda Hamaccabi is lined with local cafés and restaurants, along with a handful of small boutiques and a peaceful spa, that together exude an unmistakable feeling of community. Several of the cafés overlook Milano Square, a charming green oasis.

**Hayarkon Park**

Just a short stroll from Yehuda Hamaccabi is the city's ultimate green gem, Hayarkon Park. At nearly 4 kilometers square, the sprawling park offers endless activities for families, sports fans, history buffs, concertgoers and nature lovers. Since it opened in 1973, the park also known as Ganei Yehoshua has provided Tel Avivians with a breath of fresh air: In addition to the expansive lawns where locals rest and picnic, there are also paths for bicycling and jogging, rock and tropical gardens, a water park, a sports and recreation facility, an artificial lake, an aviary and even Ottoman-era ruins. The park also frequently hosts outdoor festivals and concerts by international celebrities, including, in recent years, Madonna, Elton John and Paul McCartney.

**North of Hayarkon Park – Ramat Aviv, Ramat Hachayal**

Since its founding in 1909, Tel Aviv has continued to develop and build at a frenetic pace. Nowhere is this more obvious than in the area north of the Yarkon River, where on any given day construction cranes can be seen dotting the landscape and fences border new construction sites. Starting in the 1950s, after the 1948 Arab-Israeli War, Tel Aviv began to expand north of the river and cultivate new neighborhoods—ones that today form the various sections of Ramat Aviv.

While the entire north end is generally viewed as prosperous, Ramat Aviv—and its gleaming white housing developments with manicured gardens—is undoubtedly upper class. This area is home to the Ramat Aviv Mall, one of the city's most exclusive shopping centers, and also to Tel Aviv University. The university campus can be accessed from Haim Levanon Street, where the Diaspora Museum and the Eretz Israel Museum are also located. The former, which is on university grounds and traces the 2,500-year history of the exile

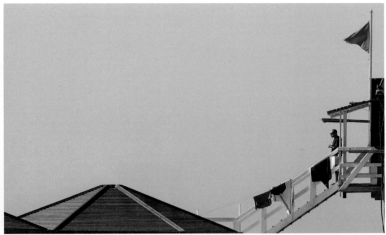

of the Jewish people using exhibitions and multimedia displays, is an engrossing place to visit. The Diaspora Museum also offers visitors interested in genealogy the opportunity to search a computerized database of thousands of genealogies of Jewish families from all over the world. The Eretz Israel Museum, meanwhile, showcases works from fields such as archaeology and Judaica, and devotes pavilions to ancient glass, coins and ceramics. Its gift shop offers a unique array of original handcrafted wares produced by leading Israeli designers and craftsmen.

East of Ramat Aviv is the neighborhood known as Ramat Hachayal, which was also established after the 1948 war as a residential neighborhood featuring small cottages. Today the area houses Israel's largest private hospital, Assuta, and is more representative of Israel's burgeoning high-tech industry with its sleek office buildings and fashionable restaurants, bars and live-music venues.

# TOLLMAN'S ALESSI

G Tzameret
10 Nisim Aloni St.
Tel. (03) 534 7025
*Map/Carte 1*

# TOLLMAN'S

71 Ibn Gvirol St.
Tel. (03) 522 3236
www.tollmans.co.il

For more than 20 years, the name Tollman's has been synonymous with high-end, cutting-edge design. The company, which has seven stores across the country and two in Tel Aviv, has no peer in terms of the designer furniture and housewares it offers and also in terms of the staff's knowledge about the international design market. Tollman's displays the works of more than 200 groundbreaking designers and represents more than 30 of the world's most prominent brands. One of those brands, the 90-year-old design firm Alessi, recently partnered with Tollman's to launch its flagship store in Israel. Tollman's Alessi—a 250-square-meter sleek, luminous space—was designed by Raphael Navot as a light, clear and dynamic setting to highlight the formal, material and colorful Alessi collection. Tollman's Alessi places an emphasis on design as a way of life, and it offers visitors a vibrant, sensory shopping experience. The boutique follows a circular logic that draws visitors in to the heart of the space, where rings of Plexiglas display iconic pieces designed for Alessi, while furniture and larger pieces are showcased along the outer edges. The store also carries a selection of international design books, and screens films on plasma televisions about contemporary designers and the stories behind their creations.

# HEARTBREAKER

203 Dizengoff St.
Tel. (03) 522 0131
www.heartbreaker.co.il
*Map/Carte* **2**

Centrally located along Tel Aviv's most
fashionable thoroughfare, Heartbreaker
specializes in premium casual fashion.
Heartbreaker is about style and attitude and,
above all, comfort. Heartbreaker's aesthetic
can be described as cool yet effortless,
sophisticated yet low-key, relaxed yet
desirable. Designer Ori Fisherman created
the brand about five years ago and recently
opened this inviting flagship boutique. The
collection includes a variety of slouchy
T-shirts, baby-soft tank tops, delicate knits,
skinny trousers, flattering elastic-waist pants
and sheer, loose little dresses. Fisherman uses
a mostly monochromatic palette of greys
and other pale colors, but she spices it up
with touches of leopard print and tattoo-like
embroidery. To achieve the desired washed-
out look, almost each piece undergoes
dyeing, stone washing and other processes
that make every one unique. In addition
to its own line, Heartbreaker offers belts,
shoes, leather bags and jewelry by Israeli and
international designers.

# DORI CSENGERI
242 Dizengoff St.
Tel. (03) 604 3273
www.doricsengeri.com
*Map/Carte 3*

In her small, Parisian-style store, internationally celebrated designer Dori Csengeri offers a collection of exquisite hand-embroidered jewelry. Dori fuses her background in textile design and the arts with impeccable craftsmanship to create stunning haute couture and ready-to-wear pieces. Each of Dori's awe-inspiring designs is hand-sewn at her Tel Aviv atelier by experienced embroidery artisans. The pieces are sensual, surprisingly lightweight and are backed with leather for the wearer's comfort. Dori's designs include an exuberantly diverse array of styles, from elegant casuals to sleek classics, and all of them speak to sophisticated, independent women who enjoy standing out from the crowd. Dori's work also features a capsule collection that offers modern men an abundance of versatility in trendsetting style. Dori Csengeri's creations are presented worldwide in prestigious jewelry stores and galleries, and are regularly featured in leading fashion and lifestyle magazines.

# JEREMIAH

306 Dizengoff St.
(corner of Yirmiyahu St.)
Tel. (077) 793 1840
*Map/Carte 4*

Jeremiah has long been a favorite café among locals looking for a neighborhood hangout where the atmosphere is funky yet laid-back, the coffee is just right and the food is top-notch. This welcoming café on North Dizengoff, not far from the port, is the perfect place to pass time—whether you just want a quick breakfast or you need to camp out with your laptop and spend hours working. Jeremiah serves up distinctly Israeli home-style food, including classic shakshuka, chopped liver, spicy Moroccan fish and luscious desserts. Oh, and don't forget to check out the PlayStation in the upstairs gallery.

## SHILA

182 Ben Yehuda St. • Tel. (03) 522 1224

One of the finest bar-restaurants in Tel Aviv, Shila's young, talented Chef Sharon Cohen serves up Catalonian-influenced seafood and tapas using the freshest ingredients.

## 223

223 Dizengoff St.

This welcoming cocktail bar features décor inspired by the 1940s—including bartenders in suspenders. It gets crowded on weekends, but is the perfect place for an intimate mid-week date.

## ALKALAY

1 Alkalay St. • Tel. (03) 604 1260

Alakalay is a neighborhood café whose proprietors also own the wine bar/shop next door featuring relaxed outdoor seating in the charming Basel area.

## ARMANI CASA

3 Hata'arucha St. • Tel. (03) 544 3306

Located near the Tel Aviv Port, this flagship store carrying the famed Italian designer's housewares caters to Tel Aviv's bourgeois crowd.

## BANKER

210 Dizengoff St. • Tel. (03) 529 0358

One of the most popular boutiques on posh north Dizengoff, Banker is beloved for its chic and funky, and mostly imported, European style.

## BARBUNIA

163 Ben Yehuda St. • Tel. (03) 527 6965

Aptly named for a common local fish, this popular restaurant serves up grilled fish and seafood accompanied by freshly made salads in a lively atmosphere that includes alfresco seating.

## BAR BARBUNIA

192 Ben Yehuda St. • Tel. (03) 524 0961

Located steps away from the restaurant of the same name, Bar Barbunia is nearly always packed with a diverse crowd the space with good vibes while enjoying delicious, simply prepared seafood dishes washed down with a cold beer.

## BOYA

Tel Aviv Port • Tel. (03) 544 6166

One of the most popular spots at the port, Boya is the perfect place to watch the sunset while enjoying a chilled glass of wine and some light Mediterranean fare.

## DEVIDAS

1 Yehuda Hamaccabi St. • Tel. (03) 602 1602

A specialty store for Tel Aviv's cigar connoisseurs.

# FABLAB FABIANI
280 Dizengoff st.
Tel. (03) 602 5569
www.fablabfabiani.com
*Map/Carte* **5**

The eye-catching, conceptual window displays at FabLab Fabiani provide the first hint that it is one of Tel Aviv's more distinctive boutiques—and this notion is confirmed once you step inside the meticulously designed space. On one side of the boutique, rows of beautifully crafted leather shoes and boots rest in sleek white display cases, while the other side of the shop showcases avant-garde yet wearable garments for women in a muted palette, alongside leather handbags, sunglasses, jewelry and perfume. Since opening in 2002, FabLab Fabiani has cultivated a reputation for its bold, cutting-edge collections, which combine unique pieces from 30 international designers that are selected with great care. FabLab Fabiani appeals to women of all ages who are intellectual and confident and, above all, seek an innovative approach to the body, along with revolutionary ideas that expand their creative horizons and minimize the gap between art and fashion.

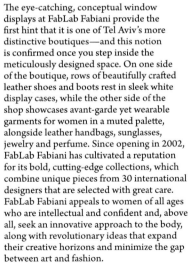

# YAEL HERMAN
211 Dizengoff St.
Tel. (03) 522 1816
Mobile (052) 367 6647
www.yaelherman.com
Map/Carte **6**

Jewelry designer Yael Herman showcases her creations in a stark white space that has the distinct feel of a gallery. Inside, rectangular and pyramid-shaped glass cases house her designs: contemporary pieces composed of 18k and 24k gold, silver and stainless steel, some of which are adorned with diamonds. Herman's designs often have a playful quality to them, and her collections are inspired by everything from tic-tac-toe to origami to Zen stone gardens. Each piece is a three-dimensional work of art that complements its wearer's essence. It comes as no surprise, then, that Herman's work has been exhibited at international galleries and museums, including New York's Museum of Arts and Design, and has been featured in design titles, such as *500 Gemstone Jewels* and *500 Plastic Jewelry Designs.*

---

## GERTRUD
225 Dizengoff St. • Tel. (03) 546 7747

This lovely boutique focuses on romantic fashion and lingerie crafted from natural fabrics that are feminine and flattering.

## GAZOZ
Hangar 1, Tel Aviv Port

Known for its winning location and exclusive design, Gazoz is a super sleek mega bar that features an outdoor patio and refreshing summer breeze.

## GILLY'S
Tel Aviv Port • Tel. (03) 605 7777

Originally a Jerusalem institution, Gilly's serves excellent food in a lovely waterfront setting with a spectacular view. The lavish breakfasts are a highlight.

---

## ICEBERG VOLCANO
Tel Aviv Port • Tel. (03) 602 6000

Widely considered one of the best ice cream parlors in Israel, Iceberg offers all the classic flavors along with inventive varieties such as honey banana and unusual fruit sorbets. Presided over by Chef Yaron Laurent, this branch, also a pizzeria, serves delicious crispy pizza if you're in the mood for a meal before dessert.

## LULU CAFÉ PATISSERIE
5 Alkalay St. • Tel. (03) 602 0805

A charming café in the heart of the Basel Square area, Lulu is the perfect place for a casual lunch or a heartly breakfast on Friday mornings.

## GALINA
Tel Aviv Port • Tel. (03) 544 5553

One of the city's hottest mega bars, Galina faces the Mediterranean and is regularly packed with beautiful people who go there to see and be seen.

---

## MOVIEING CAFÉ
25 Yirmiyahu St. • Tel. (03) 544 4708

A fun neighborhood café that includes a DVD library.

## MUL YAM
Tel Aviv Port • Tel. (03) 546 9920

Meaning "facing the sea," Mul Yam offers superb seafood, wine and ambience, with prices to match.

## IDELSON 10
252 Ben Yehuda St. • Tel. (03) 544 4154

Named for its original, now defunct location on Idelson Street, this café is renowned for its delectable cakes and pastries, including its famous cremeschnitte.

## STORY

246 Dizengoff St.
Tel. (03) 544 8911
*Map/Carte 7*

Appropriately located at the intersection of two popular shopping destinations—Dizengoff and Basel Streets—Story offers ultra-cool Tel Avivians contemporary fashion and accessories from some of the hottest global brands. Story is the retail arm of 911 Fashion, a firm with exclusive import rights in Israel to a number of international labels, including Fornarina, Nudie Jeans, Melissa, Goliath, Religion, Prim I Am, Shoe the Bear and Junk de Luxe. The boutique's name stems from the belief that each brand has a story, and the shop carefully selects each piece in order to create a well-balanced mix of clothing, shoes and accessories for men and women—all under one roof. The space itself is equally innovative, featuring funky displays and background music, and the friendly salespeople are professional and attentive. Fashion hounds can also find samples from previous seasons at Short Story, a nearby outlet at 173 Dizengoff Street.

# INN7

177 Ben Yehuda St.
Tel. **(03) 620 1022**
www.inn7.co.il
*Map/Carte 8*

INN7 is the retail arm of an Israeli firm of the same name that holds exclusive import and distribution rights to a number of leading brands from all over the world. Specializing in innovative, contemporary fashion, INN7 is a high-fashion multi-brand concept boutique that offers in-the-know locals clothing, shoes and accessories from sought-after designers. The impressive 200-square-meter boutique is nestled in a basement space along Ben Yehuda Street in ritzy north Tel Aviv. Since opening in 2008, INN7 has become one of the best-kept secrets among the city's elite: Fashionistas, stylists, celebrities, actors, musicians and media personalities all come here for their fix of cutting-edge, expertly crafted fashion: Belgian favorite Raf Simons, English classic Fred Perry, the rock-and-roll inspired Danish line Gestuz, Finnish fashion-art brand Ivana Helsinki, upscale Italian labels Xacus and Danielle Alessandrini and more.

# TES LEATHER BAGS
33 Basel St.
Tel. (03) 560 1482
www.tesbags.com
*Map/Carte 9*

TES stands for Tali Epstein Segal, the designer that created this brand of chic yet functional leather handbags and accessories. The vast world of the arts serves as the inspiration for Epstein Segal's pieces, which feature refined shapes, clean lines and buttery leather, mainly in rich hues of brown, black, blue and grey. TES' bags—including large and medium handbags, messenger bags, satchels and backpacks—are displayed along steel pipes at her flagship boutique, which features minimalist décor but still exudes warmth. The collection's distinctive designs have brought it international attention, landing it in the pages of leading fashion magazines and on television's *The L Word*, as well as on the shelves of boutiques worldwide.

## ROSA PARKS
265 Dizengoff St. • Tel. (03) 544 4881

A trendy neighborhood bar that has long been a favorite among locals.

## VANIGLIA
22 Ashtori Haparchi St. • Tel. (03) 602 0185

Arguably the best ice cream in Tel Aviv, Vaniglia uses fresh, natural ingredients to create truly unique flavors. Don't be shy when it comes to asking for a taste before deciding.

## YOSEF
213 Dizengoff St. • Tel. (03) 529 8991

One of Israel's most critically acclaimed designers, Yosef Peretz concentrates on avant-garde eveningwear that blends bold colors and flowing silhouettes.

## ZORIK
4 Yehuda Hamaccabi St. • Tel. (03) 604 8858

Located near Milano Square, Zorik is a popular, casual neighborhood café that attracts a lively young clientele.

## B KNIT
238 Dizengoff St. • Tel. (03) 544 4227

If you're looking for high-quality linens and bedding or comfortable, super-soft loungewear, this is the place for you.

## SEGEV EXPRESS
38 Habarzel St. • Tel. (077) 414 2025

Despite its slightly out-of-the-way location, it's nearly impossible to get a seat at this express outlet of celebrity Chef Moshe Segev's Herzliya restaurant, whose Italian dishes are creative and healthy.

## LILAMIST
280 Dizengoff St. • Tel. (03) 544 4058

Featured in major fashion magazines and often seen on celebrities, Lilamist's evening gowns combine colorful, extravagant colors and patterns with the highest-quality fabrics and superior attention to detail.

## MEL & MICHELLE
155 Ben Yehuda St. • Tel. (03) 529 3232

This intimate Italian restaurant is the perfect choice for a romantic dinner, as it combines pleasant ambience, superb authentic cuisine, an excellent wine list and some of the best desserts in the city.

## SUZIE BERGMAN
21 Yirmiyahu St. • Tel. (077) 632 9031

Casually chic clothes for the quintessentially Tel Aviv woman.

# MAYU OUTLET

209 Dizengoff St.
Tel. (03) 522 2877
www.mayu.co.il
Map/Carte 10

Following the success of her three previous boutiques, designer Maya Zukerman recently opened her fourth installment of Mayu, which serves mainly as an outlet, along bustling Dizengoff Street. Fans of Mayu's casual-chic aesthetic, master craftsmanship and delicate palette can find a bounty of it here. The minimalist shop stocks pieces from Zukerman's in-house line, along with select pieces from other local favorites, including Karin:A, Hoko, Meytal Sasson, Q, Nona Elga and others. Mayu also offers select items imported from designers in France and Italy, who share its devotion to sophisticated simplicity and high-quality textiles that are comfortable and universally flattering.

### EDNA
52 Yirmiyahu St. • Tel. (03) 628 9000

This mythological restaurant from Ramat Hasharon finally opened a branch in Tel Aviv, where you can treat yourself to simple but delicious home-style food at affordable prices.

### TONY VESPA
267 Dizengoff St. • Tel. (03) 546 0000

The motto at this insanely good pizza parlor is "eat as much as you like and pay accordingly." It's amazing no one's ever thought of that before.

### MAYA NEGRI
132 Jabotinsky St. • Tel. (03) 695 5133

Fashion designer Maya Negri creates high-quality garments that are comfortable and flattering, and equally perfect for a business meeting or gallery opening.

### ALUMA
9 Ashtori Haparchi St. • Tel. (03) 604 6095

*Time Out* recently named this boutique the best in Tel Aviv. Named for designer Aluma Klein, the shop carries cutting-edge, exquisitely crafted evening wear and separates and the store itself has also become a showcase for local artists and designers.

### LA GATERIE
184 Ben Yehuda St. • Tel. (077) 218 0077

This tiny gem of a place serves buttery croissants stuffed with a variety of fillings, including gourmet sausages, meats and cheeses topped with a poached egg. Paired with coffee or a glass of wine, La Gaterie's sandwiches are the perfect snack, day or night.

### TURKIZ
Sea & Sun Beach • Tel. (03) 699 6306

Located in Ramat Aviv and overlooking the Mediterranean, Turkiz mostly caters to business people and ladies who lunch, and offers the freshest fish and seafood dishes, along with a wine list of more than 2,000 selections.

### BAR HANEVI'IM
54 Yirmiyahu St. • Tel. (03) 605 6575

This well-liked neighborhood joint is packed every night thanks to its winning mix of good music, quality drinks and casual vibe.

### JUNO
1 De Haas St. • Tel. (03) 544 6620

Located near Milano Square, Juno is a super cozy wine bar with no more than ten tables, where couples looking for an intimate evening can share a bottle of wine and some tasty small plates.

### ADORA
226 Ben Yehuda St. • Tel. (03) 605 0896

This bistro run by Chef Avi Biton is consistently praised for its innovative French fare that is infused with a Mediterranean twist. Biton is renowned for his use of local ingredients and spices, in creative dishes such as his signature foie gras baklava.

# BLUE BANDANA

52 Hei BeIyar St.
Tel. (03) 602 1686
*Map/Carte 11*

The owners of Blue Bandana have high standards for the eclectic home accessories they carefully handpick for their welcoming shop: If an item isn't worthy of being displayed in their own homes, then it's not good enough for their clients. The two women, Betty Gehorsam, who grew up in Australia, and Limor Gorali, who was raised in the United States and Brazil, apply their international sensibility when selecting individual pieces at design and houseware exhibitions worldwide. Unassuming aluminum shelves allow the unique wares to take center stage: delicate multicolored crystal goblets sit alongside ceramic dishes in rich hues of purple and green; Asian-influenced vases and sculptures rest next to plush knit blankets; floral tablecloths burst with color, while a small display showcases distinctive jewelry. If you don't have time to globetrot, shopping here will certainly make you look like you do.

# RONIMOTTI
24 Raoul Wallenberg St.
Tel. (03) 647 0247
www.ronimotti.com
Map/Carte **12**

Nestled within the high-tech bubble of Ramat Hachayal is the intimate enclave of Ronimotti, which takes its name from chefs and partners Roni Belfer and Motti Sofer. This pleasantly elegant Italian restaurant serves delicious breakfasts, and is a great spot for a business lunch or romantic dinner. Belfer and Sofer pour equal measures of love and expertise into their handmade pastas and baked goods, which are all made on the premises. Ronimotti also serves fresh salads, a variety of flavorful sausages and Italian standards such as antipasti and carpaccio. The restaurant, which is open seven days a week, includes a small shop selling a wide variety of gourmet Italian food and wine, and also offers delivery service.

## SPADA
Tel Aviv Port • Tel. (03) 544 5775

A spacious showroom offering upscale housewares and bath accessories from renowned designers.

## SEATARA
Sea & Sun Beach • Tel. (03) 699 6633

Located in a residential Ramat Aviv building opposite the Mediterranean, Seatara offers guests a pleasant indoor atmosphere for enjoying the magical view and an outdoor terrace, where they can feel the natural sea breeze. There's also an extensive bar with a large variety of special cocktails.

## YULIA
Tel Aviv Port • Tel. (03) 546 9777

A solid seafood restaurant in a great location, Yulia is a wonderful spot to enjoy a glass of wine while gazing out at the sea.

## ELIEZER
186 Ben Yehuda St. • Tel. (03) 527 5961

Perpetually crowded, this small, often smoky neighborhood bar is a haven for hipsters who like the casual atmosphere and indie-alternative soundtrack.

## HAGAR SATAT
37 Basel St. • Tel. (03) 602 3718

Hagar Satat redefines the concept of jewelry with her inspiring designs that blend interesting textures and materials.

## BABY TEVA
231 Dizengoff St. • Tel. (03) 529 0910

Meaning "nature baby," this shop specializes in toys, clothes, beauty products and other items for babies and their families, all made from natural fabrics and materials.

## BANOT – LOULOU LIAM
212 Dizengoff St. • Tel. (03) 529 1175

This boutique is one of the ultimate spots in the city for soft, feminine and sexy eveningwear, bridal gowns and lingerie.

## FARMERS' MARKET
Tel Aviv Port • Tel. (077) 549 3094

Conceived by food journalist and television presenter Michal Ansky, this open-air market features 50 vendors from all over Israel, who sell their fresh, quality produce that is grown locally on a small scale. You can find an incredible array here: fruits, vegetables, herbs, cheese, bread and cakes, honey, olives and olive oil, halva and tehina, wine, beer and flowers.

## LEONARDO BOUTIQUE
17 Habarzel St. • Tel. (03) 511 0066

Located in the high-tech hub of Ramat Hachayal, this 167-room hotel has a view of the entire city and combines urban adventure, breathtaking design and luxury.

*Jewelry • Bijoux*

## LAHOVER SHAY & ADI

203 Dizengoff St.
Tel. (03) 523 3887
www.shay-lahover.com
*Map/Carte 2*

Over the last 25 years, Shay Lahover has become one of Israel's leading jewelry designers, with the quality of his exquisitely wrought pieces placing him among the country's finest artisans. Lahover and his partner, Adi, use pure 22k and 24k gold to craft ornate rings, earrings, necklaces, bracelets and brooches. Their unique designs are inspired by nature, art, archaeology or legends; each one-of-a-kind piece emerges from an idea that is then molded into a richly detailed composition. The pieces feature inlaid precious and semi-precious stones and gems in a spectrum of vibrant colors, while some also combine platinum. Their designs often contain contradictions that somehow seem to work together: They are simultaneously substantial and delicate, raw and refined, trendy and timeless. To glimpse these striking works, stop by the inviting shop on Dizengoff—it's the one with the colorful bangles adorning the door.

# LUCK
5 Alkalay St.
Tel. (03) 544 2252
www.luckworld.co.il
*Map/Carte 13*

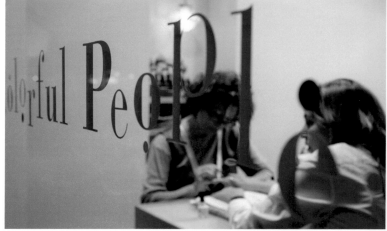

Luck, a mini spa located in the quaint Basel Square area, specializes in providing pampering beauty treatments in a nurturing, relaxing environment where cell phones are unwelcome. Luck's holistic approach encourages clients to unwind by treating their bodies and soothing their souls. The spa's qualified, experienced team of beauty professionals offers a wide range of treatments, including manicures, medical and cosmetic pedicures, foot massages, hair removal and a new line of facials—all of which are accompanied by calming music, fragrant scents and, of course, a smile. Whether you pop in for a quick manicure or indulge in Luck's signature Nirvana foot massage and a nourishing anti-aging facial, your experience will leave you feeling rejuvenated and refreshed. Luck also offers gift certificates that are perfect for a loved one, and hosts private events such as bachelorette and birthday parties.

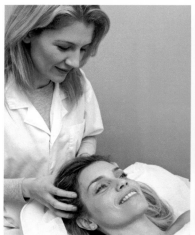

*hotel • hôtel*

# SHALOM HOTEL & RELAX

216 Hayarkon St.
Tel. (03) 762 5400
www.atlas.co.il
*Map/Carte 14*

Designed as a beach house and located just steps away from Tel Aviv's promenade and rolling waves, the recently opened Shalom Hotel caters to guests who enjoy being pampered. The boutique hotel offers 51 air-conditioned rooms decorated in a relaxed Mediterranean style. Some rooms include attractive and spacious sitting areas while others feature stunning beach views. The romantic and luxurious spa rooms include a private Jacuzzi from which guests can gaze out at the magnificent surroundings. Other amenities include free in-room computer and WiFi, flat-screen television, hot beverage corner, mini refrigerator and safe suitable for a laptop. Shalom Hotel also offers complimentary bicycle rentals and upscale refreshments, including a selection of teas and infusions. The hotel's crowning gem is its rooftop lounge, where guests relax in rocking chairs—the perfect spot from which to watch the sunset.

# GOLDY

232 Dizengoff St.
Tel. (03) 544 6149
www.goldy-tlv.co.il
*Map/Carte 15*

The first thought likely to cross your mind upon entering Goldy is: Where should I look first? This charming jewelry and accessories shop offers a diverse array of necklaces, earrings, bracelets and rings, designed by dozens of Israeli artisans, as well as an assortment of handbags, wallets, scarves and hats. The jewelry on display ranges from gold, silver, gold-plated and gold-filled pieces to items crafted from different metals, leather and plastic—and the styles are equally varied. Romantic and vintage pieces rest alongside modern, trendy and more industrial ones. Goldy is an ideal spot to find a gift for a loved one and, yes, that includes you.

## SHUSHU
20 Yirmiyahu St.

"Shushu" in Hebrew means keeping something on the down low—and that's the perfect phrase for describing this trendy underground bar, which you enter through the frozen yogurt shop on Ben Yehuda and Yirmiyahu Streets.

## FU SUSHI
32 Yirmiyahu St. • Tel. (03) 605 1000

This relative newcomer has already garnered a reputation for serving up some of the freshest sushi and Japanese food in a dynamic, modern atmosphere. In other words, be prepared for a wait.

## RAK BASAR
14 Raoul Wallenberg St. • Tel. (03) 644 4833

Meaning "only meat," this innovative restaurant offers a unique dining experience: Diners take a number, choose their cut of meat from the butcher and the staff prepares it at your table while you watch—and drool.

## UMBRELLA
252 Dizengoff St. • Tel. (03) 546 3867

Umbrella is a collective designer shop offering contemporary clothing and accessories from a variety of local talents, all under one roof—hence the name.

## RUBEN
32 Yirmiyahu St.

Taking its name from the classic sandwich, Ruben was the first to bring traditional New York–style deli fare to Tel Aviv. The restaurant is an ode to smoked meats, which it serves on fresh bread, with pickles, sauerkraut or spicy sauce.

## HEMDA
109 Ibn Gvirol St. • Tel. (074) 702 4664

This bright, cozy bakery-café offers a full breakfast menu including shakshuka and muesli, but what people mainly come here for is the sweets: cakes and pies in dozens of varieties, along with sweet and savory pastries, all of which are to die for.

## ROKACH 73
73 Rokach St. • Tel. (03) 744 8844

Tucked away behind tennis courts in Hayarkon Park, Chef Eyal Lavi's charming restaurant offers classic Provençal cuisine with a Mediterranean twist, using the freshest seasonal ingredients.

## ERETZ ISRAEL MUSEUM SHOP
2 Haim Levanon St. • Tel. (03) 641 5244

Located at the entrance to the museum in Ramat Aviv, the gift shop is a spacious, elegant emporium renowned throughout the country for its diverse array of high-quality traditional and contemporary Israeli decorative art and design objects.

## SUSHI SAMBA TLV
27 Habarzel St. • Tel. (03) 644 4345

The Tel Aviv outpost of this successful international brand, Sushi Samba is a colorful, sleek and sexy restaurant-bar that serves innovative Japanese-Brazilian fusion cuisine.

# AGADIR

3 Hata'arucha St., Tel Aviv Port
Tel. (03) 544 4045

2 Nahalat Binyamin St.
Tel. (03) 510 4442

120 Ben Yehuda St.
Tel. (03) 522 7080

Delivery: *5690
www.agadir.co.il
*Map/Carte 16*

Since opening its first branch more than a decade ago, Agadir has become the go-to destination for the best burger in Tel Aviv. Agadir upgraded the traditional hamburger from fast food to gourmet by offering it in varying sizes and with creative toppings, such as goose breast or goat cheese. The eclectic menu also features starters including merguez sausages and homemade Moroccan cigars as well as healthier options like veggie burgers. The chain is equally inventive with décor: The Nahalat Binyamin outpost is intimate yet modern; the larger port location features an enormous wooden bar, cozy couches and an outdoor deck; and the recently launched Agadir Embassy on Ben Yehuda is styled after a VIP room at a club and features a new, exclusive menu. If you feel like staying in, Agadir delivers its food in uniquely designed packaging well into the night.

# CAFÉ MICHAL

230 Dizengoff St.
Tel. (03) 523 0236
www.cafemichal.rest-e.co.il
*Map/Carte* **17**

Since opening in 2003, Café Michal has served as a friendly, light-filled haven where one can escape the hustle and bustle of Dizengoff Street. The café-bistro is renowned for its tasty home-style food, and its varied menu includes multiple breakfast options, hearty salads, sandwiches and main courses, an extensive dessert menu and seasonal specials that are served in the evening. Café Michal's décor, which blends European and vintage influences to create a warm, relaxed atmosphere, is equally inviting. Artists, writers and celebrities can frequently be spotted at Café Michal, but the vibe here is unpretentious and the waitstaff is always polite and attentive.

# MELODY HOTEL

220 Hayarkon St.
Tel. (03) 521 5300
www.atlas.co.il
*Map/Carte* **18**

Overlooking the Mediterranean and Independence Park and near the north port and Dizengoff Street, the work-and-play themed Melody Hotel caters to business and leisure travelers alike. The hotel was recently renovated, and its 55 rooms are sleek and beautifully furnished—and include multiple amenities to make visitors feel truly at home: free WiFi, flat-screen TVs and cable, DVD and mp3 players, complimentary bicycle rental, a hot beverage corner and safe large enough for a laptop. The hotel provides complimentary snacks and drinks during weekday evenings in the lobby, while the relaxed roof deck is the perfect place to lounge during warmer months.

# BAYIT BANAMAL
# COMME IL FAUT

Hangar 26, Tel Aviv Port
Tel. (03) 602 0521
Tel. (03) 717 1540 (Coola)
www.comme-il-faut.com
*Map/Carte 19*

Bayit BaNamal ("House at the Port"), the creation of veteran Israeli fashion house comme il faut, is a bright, airy and inviting space that offers visitors a combination of shopping and entertainment. The philosophy of comme il faut's design team is "fashion by women, for women," and this approach is felt throughout the complex overlooking the Mediterranean. Bayit BaNamal houses a comme il faut boutique, where you can find the firm's high-quality, comfortable and stylish garments, which are produced for women of all sizes and are crafted locally. The compound includes additional clothing, shoe and jewelry boutiques, as well as a female-centric erotica shop and a luxurious spa. The Coola spa caters to women, offering holistic face and body treatments, along with a variety of workshops, including belly dancing and meditation. Bayit BaNamal also hosts exhibitions by local artists and photographers focusing largely on feminist issues.

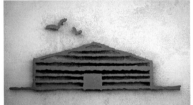

*The South • Le Sud*

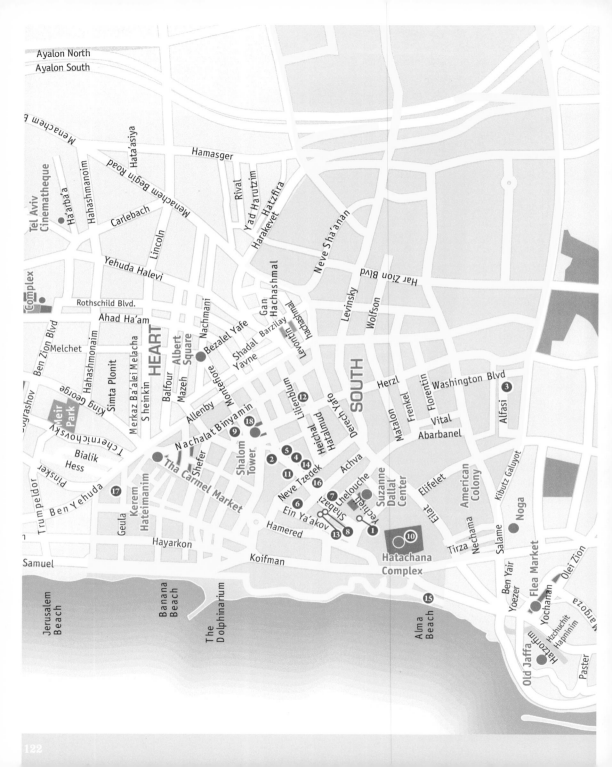

## The South • Le Sud

The south end of Tel Aviv is a splendid hodgepodge comprising varied attractions, architecture and population, which includes artists and students, Mizrachi Jews, millionaires and migrant workers from far-flung countries in Asia and Africa. This area includes several of the city's oldest neighborhoods—some of which date back more than two decades before the establishment of Tel Aviv itself—and the streets here, home to dozens of landmarks, are steeped in local lore and history.

This expansive area combines the best of old and new Tel Aviv and much of its appeal stems from that diversity: There are sparkling beaches here, including the popular Alma and Banana Beaches; a handful of vibrant markets; several remarkable synagogues as well as the recently refurbished Hassan Bek mosque, the city's only functioning mosque located outside of Jaffa; and wildly different neighborhoods including Neve Tzedek, Florentin, the Yemenite Quarter and Neve Sha'anan. Foodies will appreciate the first-rate restaurants and fine ethnic food this part of Tel Aviv has to offer, while culture enthusiasts and history buffs alike can explore the small museums, art and dance venues peppered throughout the vicinity.

Allenby Street
One of Tel Aviv's oldest streets and one of its main thoroughfares, Allenby intersects with a number of important cross-streets and connects the heart of the city to the south end. It is a hectic hub of activity that is noisy, gritty and often crowded with vehicular and pedestrian traffic. During the day, Allenby mainly serves as a low-budget shopping area, where bargain hunters pick up everything from clothing and undergarments to electrical appliances and used books in a variety of languages. The nightlife scene here consists of a couple of enjoyable restaurants, some of which have backyard seating, while the section of Allenby that runs northwest between the Carmel Market and the sea is better known for its dive bars and strip joints. Yet behind the chaotic façade exist hints of Allenby's former grandeur: Remnants of distinctive buildings from the 1920s adorned with elaborate balconies and arches; a restaurant named for a famous furrier who outfitted and threw lavish parties for Israel's rich and famous in the 1950s and '60s; synagogues with mosaic tiles bearing their architects' names; and the Tsalmania, a shop where you can buy old-time black-and-white photographs of Palestine/Israel dating as far back as the 1930s. Allenby Street is also home

to Tel Aviv's imposing Great Synagogue, which is worth a visit to catch a glimpse of the stained-glass windows that are replicas of European synagogue panes destroyed during World War II.

## Herzl Street

Named for the father of modern Zionism, Herzl Street was one of the first streets built in 1909, the year that Tel Aviv (then called Ahuzat Bayit) was established. A stroll along Herzl offers a mini history lesson on Tel Aviv's early days: This is where a number of the city's founding fathers built homes—two of which still stand at the corner of Ahad Ha'am Street. The striking structure at 16 Herzl Street was the location of Tel Aviv's first department store; inside, a faded sign points to the "ma'aliya" (an early form of "ma'alit," Hebrew for elevator), Tel Aviv's first elevator. Herzl Street is also the site of other historic buildings and momentous events. The city's first kiosk was built at the corner of Rothschild Boulevard, where a newer stall now stands; Tel Aviv's first traffic light was also erected on Herzl; and Shalom Tower, Israel's first skyscraper, was constructed on the site of the original Gymnasium Herzliya, the first school with an all-Hebrew curriculum. The mammoth building currently houses a run-of-the-mill commercial center, but the lobby holds hidden treats: two mosaic murals and miniature models of Tel Aviv in its early years.

## Lilienblum Street

Lilienblum Street, which runs perpendicular to Herzl and extends into Neve Tzedek, is also replete with history: Tel Aviv's first cinema opened here in 1913; and the building at the corner of Herzl and Lilienblum, another former founding father's home, has been painstakingly preserved and now serves as the Museum of Banking and Tel Aviv Nostalgia—fitting, as for years Lilienblum was considered Israel's financial center. Now Lilienblum is best known for the trendy bars and restaurants that bring out crowds of revelers on the weekend.

## Neve Tzedek

Established in 1887—22 years before the founding of Tel Aviv—Neve Tzedek ("Oasis of Justice") was the first neighborhood to be built by Jewish families seeking to escape overcrowded Jaffa. The prominent entrepreneur and community leader Aharon Chelouche, who immigrated to Palestine with his family from Algeria in the early 19th century, purchased land north of Jaffa's city walls and sold it to others who joined the venture. Many

of the neighborhood's streets take their names from these pioneering families, including (the misspelled) Shlush, Rokach and Amzaleg Streets, where quite a few of their original homes still stand—some even having been preserved or transformed into small museums. In the early 20th century, leading Israeli cultural figures, including Nobel Prize-winning author S.Y. Agnon and painter Nachum Gutman, also called Neve Tzedek home. Over the years, as Tel Aviv continued to expand northward, the neighborhood fell into a period of decline, only to undergo rehabilitation starting in the 1980s.

Today, Neve Tzedek, with its colorful low-rise buildings and narrow streets, is by far one of the most scenic (and expensive) sections of Tel Aviv. The Suzanne Dellal Center, a cultural venue that is home to some of Israel's top dance troupes, serves as the area's nucleus: Its European-style piazza and restored buildings are a popular meeting place for locals and tourists alike, and it's not uncommon to see brides- and grooms-to-be posing for wedding photographs against the charming backdrop. Neve Tzedek's main thoroughfare, Shabazi Street, is home to stylish boutiques selling designer clothing and upscale home decorations, along with restaurants, cafés and several pleasant wine bars.

## Hatachana (The Station Complex)

Located just steps away from Neve Tzedek, near the beachfront promenade, is the historic site of Jaffa's first train station, which was inaugurated in 1892 and connected Jaffa and Jerusalem. The municipality spent about five years restoring the original train station, train tracks and cars in order to transform the site into an entertainment and cultural complex that recaptures its former glory and bustling spirit. The compound includes a gallery, along with restaurants, cafés and a beer hall, while local Israeli designers have set up shop in most of the available retail spaces. On Friday mornings, there is a lively organic market (dubbed Orbanic, for urban organic), where you can find fresh produce, grains and other gourmet foods as well as eco-friendly handbags and beauty products.

## Nahalat Binyamin Pedestrian Mall

Nahalat Binyamin Street was originally part of a neighborhood established in 1909 bearing the same name. The long, winding road, extending from Allenby into Florentin, remains a hub for Tel Aviv's old-time textile and haberdashery stores, which share the street with newer, trendy cafés and restaurants. The portion of Nahalat Binyamin near the Carmel

Market (between Allenby and Gruzenberg Streets) is accessible only to pedestrians, and for years has hosted a popular outdoor crafts fair. Every Tuesday and Friday, artisans set up stands along the cobblestone street while buskers, jugglers and acrobats perform at various intersections along the path, adding to the festive atmosphere. The bazaar is a great place to buy handmade jewelry, glassware, paintings, ceramic crafts, Judaica, toys and other keepsakes—and for a tasty treat, indulge in a flatbread with labane and za'atar made fresh by Druze family members at a nearby stall. On other days of the week, when the pedestrian mall is less action-packed and there are fewer distractions, keep an eye out for the elegantly restored buildings and vestiges of the Eclectic architectural style.

## The Carmel Market

One of the most colorful places to visit in Tel Aviv is the city's largest market, the Carmel Market ("Shuk HaCarmel" in Hebrew), home to some of the most vibrant local sights, sounds and smells. The market's long central path and side streets burst with stalls, where lively vendors—who sometimes sing or engage in shouting duels—hawk literally everything: fresh fruits and vegetables, sweets and spices, cheeses, meat and fish, flowers, knickknacks and clothing, all at bargain prices. This is also a good place for amateur anthropologists to experience a slice of authentic life in Israel, as the customers here represent a cross-section of the population. Israelis, both Ashkenazi and Sephardic, young and old, shop here alongside new immigrants and migrant workers. The market is at its busiest, noisiest and most crowded on Friday mornings and early afternoons, when everyone descends upon it to get in last-minute shopping before the weekend.

## Kerem Hateimanim (Yemenite Quarter)

Just west of the Carmel Market is a maze of narrow streets that form the neighborhood founded in the early 20th century by immigrants from Yemen. Starting in the 1990s, the municipality began refurbishing the neighborhood's run-down infrastructure and buildings, which led to its gentrification. Today you can find students and artists, who moved here in search of affordable apartments, sharing the neighborhood with some of its more veteran residents. Tucked away among the Kerem's picturesque buildings are some of the city's most popular hummus joints and unadorned restaurants where Yemenite specialties simmer away on low flames.

Top: Florentin Neighborhood

Florentin

Dating back nearly 30 years before the establishment of the state of Israel, the Florentin neighborhood has a rich and fascinating history: Founded in the early 1920s by immigrants from Salonika, Greece, Florentin in its early days was a refuge for Jews from Greece, Turkey, Poland, Uzbekistan and North Africa. Starting in the 1930s, with encouragement from the municipality, the area also transformed into an industrial hub, and small factories and stores took up residence in many of the buildings' ground floors. The neighborhood absorbed additional waves of immigrants even after 1948, but by the 1960s the area had become neglected. Like other once-derelict parts of Tel Aviv, however, Florentin experienced something of a renaissance in the 1990s, when droves of artists and musicians seeking cheap rent relocated here, bringing with them a flurry of new cafés, restaurants, galleries and bars. The neighborhood's resurgence even became fodder for a popular television series. Directed by Eytan Fox of *Yossi & Jagger* fame, *Florentin* aired between 1997 and 2001 and followed the lives of young bohemian types.

Florentin is still considered Israel's version of New York's Lower East Side, but walking its streets you can feel the different chapters of its history converge: Derech Yafo and the surrounding streets comprise Tel Aviv's wholesale market; Wolfson and Frenkel Streets are home to lighting fixture shops and furniture stores where carpenters craft made-to-order beds and bookshelves; the lively market on Levinsky Street specializes in dried fruits and nuts, spices and pastries; Vital and Florentin Streets are the center of the area's nightlife, although a couple of excellent wine bars have opened on smaller streets such as Cordovero and Uriel Acosta, while some of the city's more frequented clubs are located along the industrial-looking outer edges of the neighborhood's Abarbanel, Comfort and Salame Streets.

## DALLAL
10 Shabazi St.
Tel. (03) 510 9292

## DALLAL – THE BAKERY
7 Kol Israel Haverim St.
www.dallal.co.il
*Map/Carte 1*

The word "Dallal" has several meanings in Arabic: prosperity, indulgence and a meeting place whose focal point is good food, among others. All of these elements reflect the essence of Dallal. The restaurant is located in a beautifully renovated late 19th-century house in the historic Neve Tzedek neighborhood. Dallal feels like three spaces in one: The outdoor patio is a lovely place to enjoy breakfast; the spacious bar is the perfect spot to order small dishes along with a chilled glass of wine; and the impeccably designed indoor space, with its cozy booths and plush chairs, is the ideal setting in which to enjoy Dallal's creative Mediterranean cuisine. The menu relies on fresh, local ingredients, and places an emphasis on meat, seafood and homemade pasta. Dallal's celebrated bread and pastries are all baked on the premises, and can be enjoyed with a coffee at Dallal – The Bakery, located around the corner from the restaurant, which thankfully also offers everything to go.

# ORIT IVSHIN
53 Shabazi St.
Tel. (03) 516 0811
www.oritivshin.com
*Map/Carte* 2

The inspiration found in the magical alleys of Neve Tzedek permeates the work of Orit Ivshin, who for more than a decade has been creating jewelry in her studio/boutique located in the historic neighborhood. Ivshin's designs are characterized by clean lines and a delicate matte finish; they also feature a unique combination of old and new, classic and contemporary. This convergence is expressed as well in the varied techniques employed by Ivshin: In addition to traditional tools such as drills, files and sandpaper, she also makes use of computer programs specializing in three-dimensional design. Ivshin's jewelry, crafted from gold and set with precious stones and diamonds, suits any woman seeking a uniquely designed piece, an individual piece like no other that will accompany the wearer over a long time.

## PRONTO
4 Herzl St. • Tel. (03) 566 0915

Modeled after authentic Italian eateries, Pronto has been a culinary and cultural institution in Tel Aviv for more than two decades. Chef Rafi Adar and business partner Ofer Zamir recently relocated Pronto to a lovely new space on Herzl Street.

*Concept Store • Magasin spécialisé*

## AHAVA
Hatachana • Tel. (03) 557 1111

If you don't have time to make it to the Dead Sea, stop by this concept store for Ahava beauty products that are rich in minerals from the salty body of water.

*Restaurant • Restaurant*

## HERBERT SAMUEL
6 Koifman St. • Tel. (03) 516 6516

Headed by renowned Chef Yonatan Roshfeld, Herbert Samuel overlooks the promenade and the Mediterranean and is packed day and night with patrons enjoying the creative, contemporary menu that includes seasonal tapas and appetizers.

*Night • Nuit*

## JAJO
47 Shabazi St. • Tel. (03) 516 4557

This tiny bar along Neve Tzedek's artsy main drag is a relaxing and magical spot for an intimate drink.

*Fashion • Mode*

## L'ETRANGER
3 Lilienblum St. • Tel. (03) 510 7101

This boutique specializing in contemporary cutting-edge fashion is the creation of a young Israeli designer who studied in Milan and whose goal is to bring the mystery of the foreign (hence the name) to Israel. Rick Owens, Giuliano Fujiwara and Forte Forte are just some of the labels found here.

*Fashion • Mode*

## SKETCH
Hatachana • Tel. (03) 962 8299

Yossi Katzav designs this exclusive men's clothing line that is created in limited editions and is inspired by the meeting point between fashion and art.

*Restaurant • Restaurant*

## ABRAXAS NORTH
40 Lilienblum St. • Tel. (03) 516 6660

Another winning restaurant from Chef Eyal Shani, Abraxas North places an emphasis on simply prepared food and straight-from-the-market ingredients. Don't miss the delicious, tender cauliflower served in parchment paper, the lovingly prepared tomato salad and the scrumptious fresh fish dishes.

*Restaurant • Restaurant*

## NG
6 Ahad Ha'am St. • Tel. (03) 516 7888

Carnivores, take note: NG serves up what are widely considered the city's best steaks.

*Restaurant • Restaurant*

## CARMELLA BISTRO
46 Hatavor St. • Tel. (03) 516 1417

Netsled in a beautiful early-20th-century building on one of the side streets near the Nahalat Binyamin pedestrian mall and the Carmel Market, Carmella is a uniquely romantic space in which to enjoy Chef Daniel Zach's lovingly prepared Mediterranean cuisine.

# KASTIEL

36 Alfasi St.
Tel. (03) 683 6334
www.kastiel.com
*Map/Carte 3*

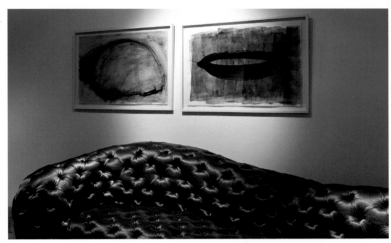

Founded in 1942 by Efraim Kastiel, the design firm bearing his name started out as a small upholstery workshop that outfitted the first Knesset seats and furnished the homes and offices of Israel's leaders and bourgeoisie. Kastiel grew to become a design institution that for decades has been considered Israel's preeminent source for custom-made furniture and accessories. Today the family-run business includes a network of upholstery, metal and carpentry workshops, all of which operate near Kastiel's impressive 3,500-meter showroom housed in a renovated Bauhaus building. There, visitors can catch a glimpse of Kastiel's custom-designed and expertly crafted pieces that are manufactured locally and supplied to clients both in Israel and abroad. The enormous space showcases furniture for indoors and out; a selection of elaborately designed area rugs; sleek accessories made from glass, porcelain and various metals; luxurious textiles and bedding; and original works of art. The renowned Kastiel design team works with clients in Israel and internationally to create striking spaces that combine the highest-quality raw materials with inimitable style and, in some cases, a touch of humor.

# ANITA ICE CREAM
42 Shabazi St.
Tel. (03) 517 0505
3 Florentin St.
Tel. (03) 683 8730
*Map/Carte 4*

Siblings Adi and Nir Avital founded this delectable ice cream parlor nine years ago, after a trip to northern Italy inspired them to bring European-style gelato and sorbet to Neve Tzedek. Anita's refreshing sorbets and unusual ice creams use only the finest ingredients and, in some cases, blend them with decadent sweets, including Kinder Bueno and cakes baked by the owners' mother. Those looking to indulge in a healthier treat can head to the 23 Shabazi Street location for low-fat frozen yogurt with assorted toppings. The shops' offerings change daily, so there are plentiful options for satisfying your sweet tooth.

### JAJO VINO
44 Shabazi St. • Tel. (03) 510 0620

Located across the street from Jajo, this cozy wine bar seats about 15 and is the ideal setting for a romantic or after-work drink.

### BELLINI
6 Yehieli St. • Tel. (03) 517 8486

Located in the picturesque Suzanne Dellal courtyard, Bellini lays on the Italian charm with its rustic red-and-white tablecloths and traditional, tasty food.

### ABRAXAS
40 Lilienblum St. • Tel. (03) 510 4435

One of the pioneers of the nightlife scene on Lilienblum Street, Abraxas remains one of the more popular bars in the city where the lively crowd often gets its groove on.

### ARIK BEN SIMHON
110 Nahalat Binyamin St. • Tel. (03) 683 7865

Arik Ben Simhon is a Tel Aviv-based furniture designer who's known for bold pieces that draw their influences from contemporary culture and even sports.

### BABETTE
31 Shabazi St. • Tel. (03) 510 0534

Catering to fashionable moms and babies in Neve Tzedek, Babette specializes in beautiful clothing and accessories from Petit Bateau and other top French labels.

### SAVTA ICE CREAM
9 Yehieli St. • Tel. (03) 510 5545

Meaning "grandmother" in Hebrew, Savta is a longstanding ice cream parlor in Neve Tzedek known for its delicious flavors and friendly staff that spoils kids with treats—just like their grandmas.

### HABASTA
4 Hashomer St. • Tel. (03) 516 9234

This charming little restaurant/wine bar near the Carmel Market serves excellently prepared, fresh food using ingredients—you guessed it—straight from the market.

### MENDALIMOS
102 Hayarkon St. • Tel. (050) 846 4462

This fun neighborhood bar is one of those places that suddenly became nearly impossible to get in to—likely thanks to its combination of cool people, relaxed vibe, loud music and sweet backyard.

### TALI'S
8 Ahad Ha'am St. • Tel. (03) 510 8848

This enchanting showroom presents a diverse selection of lifestyle accessories designed by proprietor Tali Sebbag or handpicked by her during travels to Europe.

# SAMY D.

Gallery - 56 Shabazi St.
Tel. (03) 516 4968
Studio - 23 Abulafia St.
www.samy-d.com
www.samy-d.blogspot.com
*Map/Carte 5*

French-born, Israel-based Samy D. is
internationally renowned for his breathtaking
ceramic works, which feature the pioneering
technique he developed combining rich hues,
14k gold and consummate craftsmanship.
The artist's gallery on Shabazi Street for
years has enticed passersby with its vibrantly
colored, eye-catching pieces: There you can
get a glimpse of Samy D.'s housewares, crafts
and artworks presented in sleek display
cases, or, if temptation strikes, special order
a dinnerware set for your home. Samy D.
also recently opened a new studio in the
Florentin neighborhood, which showcases
his larger artworks and full sets of dishware
that can be viewed by appointment. Samy D.'s
celebrated designs are collected by discerning
art enthusiasts and are displayed at leading
museums, galleries and exhibitions in Israel
and abroad. He also has been commissioned
to design custom-made items for exclusive
clients, including the breakfast service for
El Al Airlines' first class cabins and, most
recently, large-scale pieces for the five-star
Ritz-Carlton in Hong Kong.

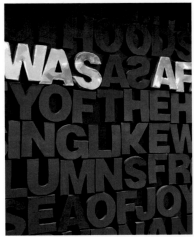

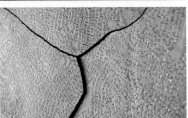

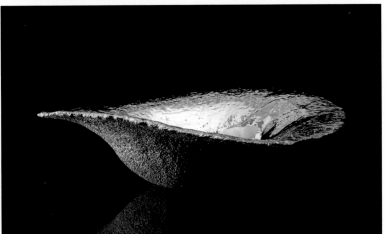

# NEVE TZEDEK HOTEL
4 Degania St.
Tel. (054) 207 0706
www.nevetzedekhotel.com
*Map/Carte 6*

Nestled within the picturesque Neve Tzedek neighborhood, this intimate boutique hotel offers a one-of-a-kind experience for guests who prefer to feel like locals during their stay. Located in a beautifully restored building dating back to 1934, the Neve Tzedek Hotel combines historic charm with contemporary design, and offers five individually decorated apartment-size suites. Artist Tommy Ben-David, who co-owns the hotel with his brother Golan Dor, designed each suite with an emphasis on natural and raw materials, including wood, concrete and steel. The suites range in size, with two featuring private gardens and Jacuzzis and two offering private balconies, while the two-room penthouse suite offers a spacious living room, private roof and Jacuzzi, espresso machine and plasma television. Hotel amenities include free WiFi, mini bar, in-room spa treatments and breakfast at the nearby Nana Bar, served daily between 9:30 a.m. and 12 p.m.

# MAYU

15 Shabazi St.
Tel. (03) 516 6975
www.mayu.co.il
*Map/Carte 7*

A few years after opening her flagship boutique near Rabin Square, designer Maya Zukerman expanded to scenic Neve Tzedek and opened shop in one of Shabazi Street's beautifully renovated 19th-century residences. Mayu's rapid expansion reflects its appeal among Tel Aviv's stylish urban women, who seek casually elegant designs made of fabrics that flatter the body and also breathe. In addition to the line designed in-house—which features a muted palette and is produced in limited editions with a focus on quality craftsmanship—Mayu also offers a selection of clothing and accessories from local and international designers. Each piece reflects Mayu's attention to expert craftsmanship and its casual-chic aesthetic that never goes out of style.

*Café • Café*

## TAZZA D'ORO
6 Ahad Ha'am St. • Tel. (03) 516 6329

Located in a beautifully restored building and patio in Neve Tzedek, this charming neighborhood café serves the finest espresso blends from Italy and is known for its decadent weekend brunch menu.

*Design • Design*

## HAFATZIM
27 Chelouche St. • Tel. (03) 517 8744

In Hebrew, "hafatzim" can mean objects or belongings, but also wishes or desires. This home accessories store combines these divergent meanings to create objects of desire, things that each of us wishes for and needs, at home and in life.

*Restaurant • Restaurant*

## CATIT
4 Heichal Hatalmud St. • Tel. (03) 510 7001

Easily one of the best restaurants in Tel Aviv, Catit offers a unique gastronomic experience, courtesy of Chef Meir Adoni, in a beautifully restored historic building in Tel Aviv. The prix fixe lunch special is a treat.

*Restaurant • Restaurant*

## NANA BAR
1 Ahad Ha'am St. • Tel. (03) 516 1915

Known for its romantic atmosphere, eclectic décor and solid bistro fare, this bar-restaurant has been a favorite in Neve Tzedek for years.

*Night • Nuit*

## SUBLET
6 Koifman St. • Tel. (054) 544 8444

This rooftop bar overlooking the Mediterranean is one of the hottest spots during the summer, when beautiful people enjoy the cool sea breeze while sipping ice-cold drinks.

*Restaurant • Restaurant*

## KIMMEL
6 Hashahar St. • Tel. (03) 510 5204

Located in a restored 129-year-old building that apparently belonged to a Turkish sheikh, this delightfully rustic restaurant has for years been dishing out traditional Provençal cuisine.

*Restaurant • Restaurant*

## PLACE FOR MEAT
64 Shabazi St. • Tel. (03) 510 4020

As its name implies, this elegant steakhouse is where carnivores can sink their teeth into a juicy cut of meat.

*Fashion • Mode*

## SKALSKI LEATHER BOUTIQUE
19 Abulafia St. • Tel. (03) 683 4505

Skalski Leather Boutique designs and manufactures luxurious, handcrafted leather accessories renowned for their attention to detail and superior craftsmanship.

*Night • Nuit*

## HAOMAN 17
88 Abarbanel St. • Tel. (03) 681 3636

First opened in an industrial area in Jerusalem, Haoman 17 later opened in an equally industrial part of Tel Aviv, where it hosts an international roster of DJs on a regular basis.

*Restaurant • Restaurant*

## SUZANNA
9 Shabazi St.
Tel. (03) 517 7580
*Map/Carte 8*

Suzanna has for years been one of the most popular spots in Neve Tzedek, due to both its tasty Mediterranean-style offerings and its scenic location in the heart of Tel Aviv's most historic neighborhood. Suzanna's lovely outdoor patio, which is shaded by an enormous ficus tree, is generally packed with diners enjoying warm and cold mezzes, stuffed vegetables, grilled fish and seafood or the café's famous kubbeh soup. During the warmer spring and summer months, the patio is graced by a cooling sea breeze, making it a pleasant spot to recharge over a cup of coffee and dessert. In the evenings between May and October, Suzanna opens its rooftop bar, where visitors can order small plates and a drink, and relax against the picturesque back-drop of Neve Tzedek and the Mediterranean.

# BROWN TLV URBAN HOTEL

25 Kalisher St.
Tel. (03) 717 0200
www.browntlv.com
*Map/Carte* **9**

Recently recommended by *The New York Times* as the place to stay in Tel Aviv, this cozy and stylish four-story boutique hotel is situated on a quiet street a stone's throw away from picturesque Neve Tzedek, the lively Carmel Market, Nahalat Binyamin pedestrian mall and action-packed Rothschild Boulevard—plus, it's just a ten-minute walk from the beach. The hotel accommodates both seasoned business travelers as well as lifestyle-conscious guests who seek easy access to Tel Aviv's vibrant city life, without an exorbitant price tag. Its design—featuring rich hues, vintage accents and works by local street artists—combines urban warmth with the faded glam of the 1970s. Its 30 rooms are intimate and well appointed. Amenities include 32-inch flat screen television, complimentary WiFi, 400 thread count linens, mini bar and laptop-size safe. The Brown TLV Urban Hotel also offers a rooftop sundeck with panoramic view, a spa suite and a business lounge for guests who insist on working.

# VICKY CRISTINA

Hatachana
Tel. (03) 736 7272
*Map/Carte 10*

Located in a scenic patio within the refurbished train station complex between Neve Tzedek and Jaffa, Vicky Cristina is a wine bar/tapas kitchen that feels like a sliver of Barcelona in Tel Aviv. The spacious courtyard, shaded by ancient ficus trees, is divided into two sections: On one side is Vicky, the tapas restaurant that opens in the afternoon hours and serves up small plates in an intimate, relaxed setting. Cristina, the wine bar, takes up the other side of the patio, and features sculpted, mosaic-covered bars inspired by renowned Spanish architect Antoni Gaudí's famous Park Güell. The wine bar opens daily at 7 p.m. and offers more than 120 wines in a festive atmosphere featuring a Spanish soundtrack. Vicky Cristina's carefully selected wine list includes an impressive array of Israeli wines that are produced at a number of excellent local vineyards, and that in recent years have garnered much international praise for their quality and flavor. Vicky Cristina consistently updates its wine list, but always with an emphasis on the best local offerings. On any given night there, guests can experience the vibrant fiesta ambiance replete with first-rate wine, sangria and ceviche.

# AGAS AND TAMAR

43 Shabazi St.
Tel. (03) 516 8421
www.agasandtamar.com
*Map/Carte 11*

The historic-yet-contemporary neighborhood of Neve Tzedek provides the ideal setting for Agas and Tamar, a jewelry line that perfectly balances past and present. More than ten years ago, designers Einat Agassi and Tamar Harel-Klein merged their names to create that of their line, which means "pear and date" in Hebrew; since then, they have honed the collection's unique style in their Shabazi Street workshop. Agassi and Harel-Klein draw influences from ancient coins, gems and precious stones, and their expertly handmade pieces express the synergy between natural materials and skilled artisanship. Agas and Tamar's collection is dedicated to the urban woman and man, and includes rings, earrings, bracelets, necklaces and cufflinks crafted from the finest matte gold and silver. The shop has long been a favorite among locals, and the popularity of its New York branch among fashionistas and celebrities attests to Agas and Tamar's solid international presence.

# NANUCHKA

30 Lilienblum St.
Tel. (03) 516 2254
*Map/Carte 12*

Nanuchka—the Georgian supper club known for its scrumptious food, strong drinks and dynamic atmosphere—has been a fixture on Lilienblum Street for years. The restaurant recently relocated to a beautiful 1930s building marked for preservation, and while the setting is new, owner Nana Shrier stayed true to the spirit, color and eclectic design that define Nanuchka. The new space features two floors: an elegant dining space, 42-seat bar and enchanting backyard take up the ground floor, while the upstairs contains an intimate dining area and colorful bar constructed out of 1,500 books, with seating that overlooks the bar below. Nanuchka's decadent style is inspired by czarist Russia, and the food reflects Georgian gastronomic culture in all its glory, with an Israeli twist. The restaurant offers lunch specials, but Nanuchka truly shines at night, when lively music fills the air and patrons dance enthusiastically on the bar.

# THE VARSANO HOTEL

16 Hevrat Shas St.
Tel. (077) 554 5500
www.varsano.co.il
Map/Carte 13

This charming boutique hotel is located within the historic and scenic Neve Tzedek neighborhood, steps away from the best of both worlds: It's just a three-minute walk to the beach and a stone's throw away from trendy boutiques, cafés, restaurants and bars. The Varsano offers savvy business travelers and those on holiday superior accommodations, including state-of-the-art amenities. Guests can choose from four different types of suites—studio, deluxe, loft or family—all of which have been carefully designed, down to the smallest details, to provide maximum comfort. The suites are spacious, well lit and feature clean, contemporary design that still exudes a homey feel. Each suite contains a fully equipped, high-end kitchen, washer/dryer, cordless phone, flat-screen television, DVD player, stereo and high-speed wireless Internet. Outside, guests can relax in the Varsano's courtyard, a private oasis that dates back more than 120 years. Guests are also invited to enjoy fine dining at the nearby Dallal culinary complex, which includes a gourmet restaurant that serves breakfast, lunch and dinner, and a French patisserie. The Varsano staff is knowledgeable and friendly, and is happy to arrange additional services for you in the suite itself or around Tel Aviv.

# SIPUR PASHUT

36 Shabazi St.
Tel. **(03) 510 7040**
www.sipurpashut.net
*Map/Carte* **14**

Founded in 2003, this independent bookstore takes its name from the Hebrew title of Nobel laureate S.Y. Agnon's novel *A Simple Story*, in which one of the characters uses books as a gateway to the world. This neighborhood mainstay—nestled among the cafés and shops of Neve Tzedek's central thoroughfare—is a favorite among bibliophiles, who come to peruse the latest Hebrew and English titles in a relaxed environment. The small space offers vast options: original and translated literature, poetry, theory and criticism, art monographs, graphic novels, children's books and periodicals. The gracious staff is knowledgeable, and always happy to make recommendations.

# BELLINKY OOLALAA

Hatachana
Tel. **(03) 736 2828**
www.bellinky.com
www.oolalaa-design.com
*Map/Carte* **10**

Taking its name from the two brands this boutique houses, Bellinky Oolalaa is an ode to inventive contemporary design. Idit and Or Bellinky create luxurious handbags and accessories as well as a limited collection of clothing. Their bags, wallets and belts are fashioned from the highest-quality leather and other fine materials imported from around the world, and their designs feature clean lines with a modern twist. Miri Ginzburg-Alony, the designer behind jewelry line Oolalaa, crafts pieces using vintage elements collected over time, as well as items that combine diverse components: a leather choker, for example, is adorned with glass stones, vintage crystals, wood and textiles. In addition to Bellinky and Oolalaa, the boutique, which is located at the heart of the renovated train station complex, also carries select items from guest designers.

# MANTA RAY

Alma Beach, near the Etzel Museum
Tel. (03) 517 4773
www.mantaray.co.il
*Map/Carte 15*

Consistently voted one of the most popular
restaurants in Tel Aviv, Manta Ray serves
up creatively prepared Mediterranean fare
against the lovely backdrop of the beach and
lapping waves. The space itself is bright and
airy, but the tables lining the outdoor veranda
and overlooking the sea are undoubtedly
the best in the house. The cuisine is equally
light and refreshing: various fish, scallops,
shrimps and squid are accompanied by side
dishes that complement but never overpower
them. The restaurant also offers meat and
poultry options, and its mezzes—small
salads and spreads featuring fresh Middle
Eastern ingredients that can be served with
Balkan bread and olive oil—have developed
something of a cult following among locals.
For those looking to get a special start to
their day, Manta Ray is also open daily for
breakfast from 9 a.m. to 12 p.m.

# ELISE

30 Shabazi St.
Tel. (03) 517 2835
25 Shabazi St.
Tel. (03) 510 9279
www.boutique-elise.com
*Map/Carte* 16

Founded in 2007 as one of Sheinkin Street's most feminine and fashionable boutiques, Elise has since expanded into a chain with four branches across Tel Aviv, and has garnered a reputation as a purveyor of timeless and unique garments. Elise Juliard imports sought-after brands from Paris and other leading European fashion capitals, and her boutique's raison d'être is to indulge and inspire women with opulent prints, luxury fabrics and polished silhouettes. Elise also offers covetable jewelry and accessories, and its recently opened shoe store is the exclusive distributor in Israel of cult brands like Repetto. If you believe that life is too short for the ordinary, welcome to the world of Elise, where every piece is a treasured favorite.

# THEODORA

51 Geula St.
Tel. (052) 360 2690
www.theodora.co.il
*Map/Carte* 17

Upon first glance, Theodora looks like a quaint store that specializes in vintage jewelry and accessories, but upon closer inspection you realize it's more than that—it's a labor of love. Proprietor Yaara Livny admittedly has a fetish for high-end designer brands as well as a deep affection for costume jewelry, both of which she channels into her feminine, pink-walled shop. Livny uses the expertise she developed in her previous work at an auction house to select the pieces for her collection, many of which are from top-tier fashion houses, including Chanel, Dior, Givenchy, YSL and Gucci. Theodora's collection also features dazzling Art Deco jewelry, along with colorful bakelite and celluloid pieces hand-picked at international markets. To enhance the classic feel, Theodora also stocks designer handbags, some dating back to the 1920s, along with sunglasses, gloves, belts and a small collection of vintage and second-hand clothing.

## MADE IN TLV
Hatachana
Tel. (03) 510 4333
www.madeintlv.com
*Map/Carte* **10**

Made in TLV is the brainchild of journalist Yuval Abramovich and television producer Dafna Dannenberg, Tel Avivans who were frustrated by the lack of aesthetic souvenirs dedicated to the place they love and call home. The duo collaborated with photographer Ziv Koren—who supplied them with spectacular shots of the city taken from unique angles—and then teamed up with designers to create a line of souvenirs that celebrate Tel Aviv. The store, which is located in the old Jaffa train station building dating back to 1892, carries the exclusive line of mementos: handbags and wallets, notebooks, puzzles, jewelry, wall decals, coat hangers and housewares that incorporate historic images of the White City.

*Design • Design*

### GAVRIEL
13 Shabazi St. • Tel. (03) 510 3882

Gavriel offers an eclectic mix of gifts and housewares carefully selected by owner Rubi Israeli from local and international designers. The shop also carries fashion by cutting-edge labels including local favorite Tom Salama.

*Night • Nuit*

### SHUSHKA SHVILI
Hatachana • Tel. (03) 516 0008

Housed in a renovated Templer home, this beer hall serves tapas and small plates that you can enjoy indoors or out, on a porch overlooking the beautifully restored train station complex between Tel Aviv and Jaffa.

*Jewelry • Bijoux*

### KEREN WOLF
1 Shabazi St. • Tel. (03) 516 1222

This feminine boutique is adored for its romantic jewelry and accessories, including bridal designs, all of which are characterized by a vintage-inspired flair.

*Fashion • Mode*

### AMERICAN VINTAGE
Hatachana • Tel. (03) 510 4441

Despite its name, American Vintage is actually a French brand beloved for its super-soft T-shirts and basics for men and women in a mostly monochromatic palette.

*Design • Design*

### ART MAROC
38 Shabazi St. • Tel. (03) 516 1326

This colorful shop makes you feel like you just stepped in to a Moroccan souk overflowing with everything from slippers to tea sets to brightly patterned tiles.

*Jewelry • Bijoux*

### HARRACA
Hatachana • Tel. (03) 641 1120

Named for jewelry designer Martine Harraca, this shop carries her artistic creations, which blend hand-sculpted and painted acrylic with sparkling Swarovski crystals.

*Night • Nuit*

### BUGSY
26 Florentin St. • Tel. (03) 681 3138

Bugsy is a café by day and bar by night, and it also happens to be a Florentin institution that attracts a loyal crowd.

*Fashion • Mode*

### BUTTERFLY
Hatachana • Tel. (03) 516 3636

After years of selling her designs at other boutiques, Butterfly creator Shirly Gruber spread her wings and opened her own space to showcase her funky, feminine wares.

*Jewelry • Bijoux*

### EFRAT CASSOUTO
Hatachana • Tel. (03) 510 7770

Efrat Cassouto designs utterly feminine jewelry and accessories inspired by Victorian, romantic and vintage aesthetics.

# HATACHANA

The old Manshiya train station,
between Neve Tzedek and the promenade
www.hatachana.co.il

*Map/Carte* **10**

After decades of being closed to the public and all but hidden from sight, the historic site of Jaffa's first train station, once a bustling commercial hub in pre-state Israel, is thriving once again thanks to a comprehensive overhaul. The complex known as "Hatachana" ("The Station") contains 22 buildings—including the train station itself, the old freight terminal and the home and factory of a German Templer family—that date back to various historical periods. A five-year renovation, down to the smallest details, transformed these structures into a picturesque contemporary site that combines history, culture and commerce. Hatachana houses a number of restaurants, cafés and bars, while local Israeli brands and designers have opened boutiques and concept stores in some of the retail spaces. The site also hosts prominent art exhibitions, along with a weekly design fair and organic market, which draw huge crowds and attest to its status as one of Tel Aviv's foremost attractions.

# HERA

30 Shabazi St.
Tel. (03) 516 9727
www.hera-jewellery.com
*Map/Carte 16*

Located in the heart of Neve Tzedek, Hera is a jewelry boutique whose classic charm stands out among the neighboring trendy and boho-chic shops. Hera's warm and welcoming atmosphere is enhanced by its combination of antique furniture, 18th-century lithographs and Art Deco–style windows. The boutique showcases the designs of Paris-bred Eva Soussana, who gained years of experience in the field working with her father, a well-known jeweler in France, from whom she also inherited her love of jewelry and unique stones. Eva infuses each piece with this passion, as well as her rich European influences and deep affinity for art and beauty. Working with 18k gold, precious and semi-precious stones, Eva's personal touch is evident at every level of the creative process. She designs each piece and carefully selects every stone in order to craft special gifts with a truly distinctive character.

# DORIT GRAY

Hatachana
Tel. (03) 604 0855
www.doritgray.com
*Map/Carte* 10

Dorit Gray has nearly 25 years' worth of experience designing and creating elegant, sophisticated jewelry that is inspired by her vivid imagination. Gray uses modern techniques to fashion necklaces, bracelets, earrings, rings and broaches out of a range of materials: 22k gold, 18k yellow gold, 14k red or white gold and sterling silver, featuring both matte and glossy finishes. Gray's work also incorporates unique precious and semi-precious stones that transform her pieces into one-of-a-kind works of art that reflect their wearer's essence. Gray's newest collection, a harmonious blend of sensuous colors and materials, can be seen at her recently opened gallery located among the shops and cafés of the scenic old train station complex near Neve Tzedek.

# HELLA GANOR

Hatachana
Tel. (03) 604 0855
www.hellaganor.com
*Map/Carte* 10

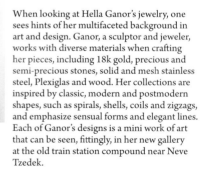

When looking at Hella Ganor's jewelry, one sees hints of her multifaceted background in art and design. Ganor, a sculptor and jeweler, works with diverse materials when crafting her pieces, including 18k gold, precious and semi-precious stones, solid and mesh stainless steel, Plexiglas and wood. Her collections are inspired by classic, modern and postmodern shapes, such as spirals, shells, coils and zigzags, and emphasize sensual forms and elegant lines. Each of Ganor's designs is a mini work of art that can be seen, fittingly, in her new gallery at the old train station compound near Neve Tzedek.

# GLORIA MUNDI

1 Ahuzat Bayit St.
Tel. (077) 460 5065
www.gloriamundi.co.il
*Map/Carte 18*

Taking its name from the Latin phrase meaning "the glory of the world," Gloria Mundi gallery celebrates just that: the world's glory. Proprietors Felix & de Vries handpick each piece during their travels around the globe, and the collection reflects a deep love and passion for aesthetics and design. Mango wood tables from Denmark, handmade iron and wood crafts from Holland, pieces from European and Colombian artisans and local contemporary art are just a few of the works found here. Some of the items have a rich history and hail from ancient castles in Europe or foreign armies. The three-story showroom is designed as a home that is divided into traditional living spaces: kitchen, living room, dining area, bedrooms and bathroom. Each showcases Gloria Mundi's unique wares: furniture, tableware, cushions, textiles, lighting fixtures and more. The shop's kitchen area also includes a café, where visitors can enjoy coffee and cake while perusing design books and magazines.

Jaffa • Jaffa

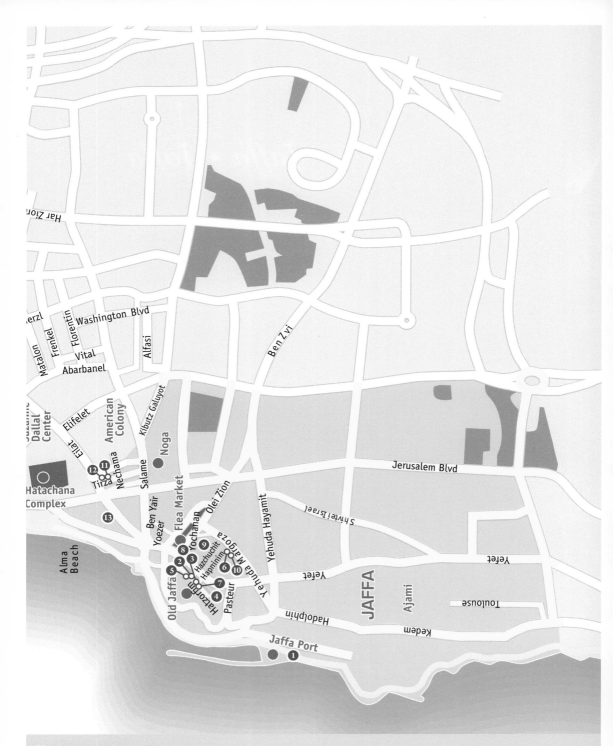

*Jaffa • Jaffa*

Jaffa (known as Yafo in Hebrew and Yafa in Arabic) is an ancient port city that is one of the oldest in the Levant. Jaffa's harbor has been in use since the Bronze Age and the city has an extensive history that includes multiple conquests, during which it was destroyed and rebuilt on more than one occasion. Jaffa is mentioned in an ancient Egyptian letter from 1470 BCE, is referred to in both the Hebrew and Christian Bibles and was the port through which King Solomon imported cedars from Tyre used to build the First Temple. Arabs conquered the city in 636 CE and the Crusaders invaded five centuries later. At various stages in its history, Jaffa has been controlled by Egyptians, Canaanites, Philistines, Persians, Phoenicians, Romans, Ottomans and Egyptian Mamluks, among others. In 1799, Napoleon's army captured and ransacked the city, which was later re-conquered by the Ottomans, who ruled it until the British take-over in 1917. For most of the 19th century, Jaffa was surrounded by walls, which were ultimately torn down to allow for expansion, and by the early 20th century, the city's mixed population of Muslims, Christians and Jews had swelled considerably. Neighboring Tel Aviv was established in 1909 as a satellite of Jaffa, and after several tumultuous decades that included the Arab Revolt of 1936-39 and the Jewish conquest of Jaffa in 1948, the two cities officially became one in 1950.

In recent years, Jaffa has experienced something of a renaissance among Tel Avivians, as the municipality has invested millions to renovate the port area and the beachfront promenade, which now connects Jaffa to Tel Aviv in the north and to Bat Yam in the south. Twenty- and thirty-something Israelis have flocked there to relocate, bringing with them new restaurants, bars and boutiques. Traditionally Arab neighborhoods including Ajami—the subject of the recent Oscar-nominated movie of the same name—have undergone gentrification, making Jaffa something of a flashpoint once again. A number of the area's majestic beachfront homes have gotten makeovers thanks to their new Jewish tenants, and poorer Arab families are slowly being priced out thanks to skyrocketing real estate costs.

Steeped in all this history (and history in the making), present-day Jaffa is a fascinating, delicately balanced mix of ancient and contemporary, Arab and Jewish, Levantine and

European—and, needless to say, it offers a wealth of things to do, see and experience: numerous landmarks and historic attractions, beautifully restored old buildings, a booming flea market and several noteworthy cultural venues.

## Jerusalem Boulevard and The Noga Quarter

Constructed in 1915 by Jaffa's Turkish-Arab Governor Hassan Bek, Jerusalem Boulevard was intended to rival Tel Aviv's grand streets, and it remains one of Jaffa's main thoroughfares, extending all the way to the entrance of Bat Yam. The boulevard, like Allenby or King George Streets in Tel Aviv, is a hectic hub of activity, often clogged with vehicular and pedestrian traffic—more so now that it has undergone an extensive renovation. The boulevard is a prime shopping destination for locals, as it is lined with grocery stores, bakeries, butchers, fish markets and small holes in the wall selling falafel or burekas and other pastries. There are also some notable historic buildings along Jerusalem Boulevard, including the area's first post office, built during the British Mandate, and Jaffa's old city hall, which is now a residential building. The renowned Gesher Theater resides at the northern end of the boulevard, on a site that used to house Noga Cinema, one of several (now defunct) movie theaters in Jaffa. Just behind the theater is the Noga Quarter, whose small streets and renovated Ottoman-era buildings are home to artists' and designers' studios as well as a few cafés and bars.

## The American Colony

Just east of the Noga Quarter, where a church steeple rises from within the patch of land connecting Jaffa to the Florentin neighborhood, lies the American Colony. In 1866, 35 Christian families set sail from Jonesport, Maine, with their belongings—and their pre-fabricated homes—to settle in the Holy Land, and established the small neighborhood characterized by wooden houses. Around the turn of the century, after suffering physical and financial hardship, the American settlers sold the colony to German Templers, which is why it is alternately called the German Colony. The remnants of the colony, including the still-active Immanuel Church and several houses, can be found on Auerbach and Bar Hoffman Streets. There you can also find the Maine Friendship House, a restored colony home that serves as a museum and is open to visitors on Fridays and Saturdays. Like other historic parts of Tel Aviv and Jaffa, the colony is now the site of a luxury residential housing project that aims to retain some of the original location's charm while transforming it for modern-day use.

St. Gregory's Church

## Old Jaffa

The silhouette of Old Jaffa, located on a hill that juts out over the Mediterranean, is one of the city's most iconic images—and one of its most beautiful. It's hard to imagine that this serene, picturesque place experienced multiple cycles of destruction and reconstruction by various forces throughout history, until it was restored starting in the 1960s and transformed into an artists' colony surrounded by cultural and historic landmarks, as well as small parks and gardens. There is plenty to explore in the scenic old city, starting at Kedumim Square, the central plaza, which is filled with archaeological artifacts, galleries, souvenir shops and restaurants, and is also home to St. Peter's Church. The square feels a bit touristy but exudes enough charm, and contains enough history, to warrant a visit. From there, the Zodiac Alleys—an intricate network of narrow streets that are home to several art galleries and studios—lead down to the refurbished port area. Old Jaffa is filled with other cultural, historic and religious landmarks that are worth exploring. Among the most notable attractions are the Libyan synagogue that dates back to 1740; the House of Simon the Tanner, an important Christian site; and Andromeda's Rock, considered the stage for a dramatic tale from Greek mythology. Art enthusiasts are encouraged to visit the Ilana Goor Museum, housed in a restored 18th-century building with stone arches and lofty ceilings, or see a production at one of the several small theaters tucked away among Old Jaffa's streets. Also recommended is one of the smallest and simplest pleasures Old Jaffa has to offer: Take a seat anywhere along the coast and gaze at the breathtaking view of Tel Aviv.

## Jaffa Port

The site of centuries' worth of history, Jaffa Port is considered the oldest functioning port in the world, where, today, fisherman still bring in the freshest catch before docking their boats at the marina. The port and surrounding warehouses had suffered neglect starting in the 1960s and stood largely vacant until a couple of years ago, when the municipality decided to renovate the area and develop it into a thriving public space. The main warehouse—a 5,500-square-meter space that once served as a packing facility for Jaffa oranges—has been transformed into a complex housing a mix of culture and commerce. Several local art galleries have opened branches at the port's pavilions, and a new salon for Palestinian art has recently moved in as well. There are a few solid restaurants in the area that offer fresh seafood and a lovely view, and Abu Hassan (a.k.a. Ali Karavan), arguably the best hummus joint in Israel, is also a short walk from here.

## Yefet Street

Running roughly parallel to Jerusalem Boulevard, Yefet is another of Jaffa's most important and most populated commercial streets. Yefet marks the eastern border of Old Jaffa and continues through the Ajami neighborhood and deeper into Jaffa all the way to Bat Yam. A stroll along Yefet Street introduces visitors to a number of Jaffa landmarks, offering a mini lesson in history, and also a glimpse into contemporary life in the residential parts of the ancient city. Starting at the northern end of Yefet is Clock Tower Square, easily one of the most visited sites in the city. Its focal point is the three-story clock tower, which was completed in 1906 to mark the 30th anniversary of the reign of Turkish Sultan Abd al-Hamid II. The tower was renovated in 1965, when colorful mosaic windows depicting events from Jaffa history were installed. The square houses several other significant Ottoman-era buildings that have been carefully restored to preserve their elaborate facades, including the *seraya*, formerly the Turkish government building, and the prison known as the *kishle*, which had served as a police station until it was bought recently by a private developer who plans to transform the site into a boutique hotel. Not far from the square is the Mahmoudia Mosque, Jaffa's largest mosque that dates back to 1812 and features an outdoor water fountain for pilgrims. Continuing south on Yefet Street leads one to the legendary Abulafia bakery. Founded in 1879, the bakery is open 24 hours a day (but closes on Passover and Yom Kippur as a gesture to its Jewish neighbors) and churns out an endless supply of savory and sweet pastries: pita bread, a calzone-type pastry called sambusac, stuffed with various cheeses or potato, as well as traditional Middle Eastern desserts like baklava and knaffe. Further south, past the flea market area, Yefet Street becomes more residential, but the area also contains some remarkable landmarks, including the Al-Kamal pharmacy, a Jaffa institution run for decades by the Geday family, as well as a number of impressive 19th- and 20th-century Christian and Western schools, churches and former hospitals.

## The Flea Market

No visit to Jaffa is complete without a stop at the bustling flea market ("Shuk Hapishpeshim" in Hebrew), whose unofficial motto could be "one person's junk is another's treasure." Located east of Old Jaffa, between Yefet Street and Jerusalem Boulevard, the market comprises a maze of mostly cobblestone streets where vendors sell everything: vintage clothing, retro housewares, black-and-white photographs and yellowing personal

Top left: Ajami Beach          Bottom Left: St. Peter's Church

documents, copper and brass antiques, beautifully refurbished mid-century modern furniture, toys, knickknacks and plenty more. You could easily spend hours sifting through all the stuff, and some shopkeepers simply invite you in to rummage through boxes and bags full of items that aren't officially on display. The market area—like other parts of Jaffa and Tel Aviv—has undergone quite rapid gentrification in recent years, as fancy new boutiques and trendy restaurants and bars have moved in, raising rents and causing concern that some of the veteran merchants will inevitably be forced to close shop. In the meantime, though, it remains a vibrant area where visitors can experience the intersection of old and new, a place offering much to see and explore, especially for those willing to get their hands a little dirty.

# JAFFA PORT
Old Jaffa Port
Tel. (03) 683 2255
www.namalyafo.co.il
*Map/Carte 1*

Jaffa Port is one of the most ancient in the world, having served as a passage for merchants, religious pilgrims, conquerors and immigrants. Throughout its nearly 5,000-year history, the port endured neglect and even destruction, which makes its modern-day incarnation as a thriving fishing harbor and public space all the more impressive. Thanks to a collaboration between local fisherman, residents and the municipality, the port, its warehouses and infrastructure have been renovated while preserving their historic character and charm. On any given day there, visitors can be seen strolling and exploring the area, while fishing nets are laid out to dry, boats bob in the water and seagulls hover overhead. Guests can enjoy scenic views of the old lighthouse and other historic sites, while the port's refurbished former warehouses offer an innovative blend of culture and commerce and a diverse array of activities. The renovated British Mandate–era hangars contain an eclectic mix of restaurants, art galleries and salons, along with the site's first boutique hotel. The port also hosts music festivals, art exhibitions and shopping events, making it one of the ultimate places to experience the city's unique blend of old and new.

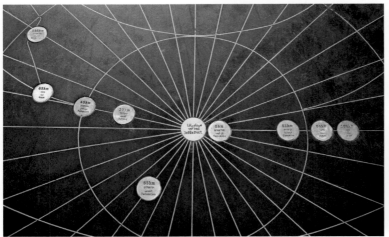

# CORDELIA

30 Yefet St. (inside the alley)
Tel. (03) 518 4668
www.cordelia.co.il
*Map/Carte 2*

Nestled in an ancient alley on the border between Old Jaffa and the flea market area is Cordelia, the flagship restaurant of celebrity Chef Nir Zook's culinary empire. Cordelia is renowned for its inventive menu—which fuses French classics with Mediterranean touches and conceptual flair—and for its equally inspired décor. The striking space, located in a centuries-old Crusader-era building, is replete with candelabras, chandeliers, mirrors, wine goblets, plush chairs and dark wood tables, all of which combine to create a romantic environment that envelops diners as they enjoy the highly imaginative cuisine. The menu at Cordelia changes frequently, as it relies on premium local and seasonal ingredients, and the unusual flavors and combinations found in each dish consistently surprise and delight guests. Those up for a truly decadent adventure are encouraged to try Cordelia's multi-course tasting menu, often cited as one of the most unique gastronomic experiences in Israel.

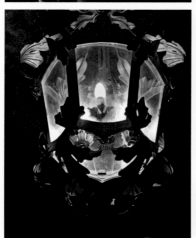

# NOA BISTRO

14 Hatzorfim St.
Tel. (03) 518 4668
www.cordelia.co.il
*Map/Carte 3*

Located just around the corner from Cordelia, Noa Bistro is another example of Chef Nir Zook's winning combination of creative cuisine and artsy ambience, but is more relaxed and affordable than its older sister. The bistro is situated in a covered alleyway known for its quirky décor, which includes dangling plants and strands of peppers hung out to dry, along with a mish-mash of flea market finds that together make for a comfortable, casually sophisticated setting. During the day, Noa Bistro is washed with sunlight, while at night the eclectic space is candle-lit, creating a more romantic atmosphere. The inventive seasonal menu focuses on Levantine favorites that are infused with French accents, and includes refreshing salads, cheeses from the Zook family farm, fresh fish and seafood and high-quality meats. Noa Bistro also offers an excellent weekend brunch and a six-dish tasting menu that won't break the bank.

# NAPOLEON PATISSERIE

15 Kedumim Sq.
Tel. (077) 403 0258
www.cordelia.co.il
*Map/Carte* 4

This newest addition to Chef Nir Zook's culinary dominion is located in picturesque Old Jaffa's central square, adjacent to the Ilana Goor Museum. Zook collaborated with pastry chef Liran Gruda to open the patisserie, which is as much as treat for the eyes as it is for the taste buds. Visitors can enjoy a coffee or tea alongside one of Napoleon's many gourmet pastries, baked goods and breads, which come in both sweet and savory varieties. The bright, airy space recalls Jaffa's rich history with its ancient stone and classic arches—and makes a perfectly serene setting from which to gaze out at the Mediterranean.

# JAFFA BAR

30 Yefet St. (inside the alley)
Tel. (03) 518 4668
www.cordelia.co.il
*Map/Carte* 5

Jaffa Bar is the third establishment to take up residence within Chef Nir Zook's "plaza," and it is set opposite Cordelia in the same enchanting ancient alley. The bar is a charming spot featuring both indoor and outdoor seating, characterized by the eclectic décor that enhances the Nir Zook culinary experience. Guests can sit in a relaxing armchair or lounge on a cozy couch and enjoy conversation over an inventive cocktail or fine glass of wine from the extensive drinks menu. The sleek bar, which attracts a sophisticated clientele, also serves reasonably priced dishes from the prolific chef's kitchen.

*Design • Désign*

# ONE BEDROOM

12 Margoza St.
Tel. (03) 683 6908
*Map/Carte 6*

Located within the thriving Jaffa flea market area, One Bedroom is a lifestyle boutique that draws inspiration from its surroundings, in which old and new converge. The boutique mimics a loft-like living space and is divided into sections—bedroom, closet, kitchen and dining area—all of which are characterized by a delicate, feminine touch. One Bedroom's cozy environment is like a mosaic of the elements that make up a woman's personal world: furniture, lighting fixtures, linens, tablecloths and dishes along with lingerie, clothing, handbags, shoes and jewelry. One Bedroom carries a mix of designer brands from Israel and abroad along with vintage, one-of-a-kind pieces found at European flea markets. It speaks to women who appreciate the beauty in subtle details, such as the way a bracelet adorns one's wrist, or the way a distinctive teapot enhances the experience of sipping tea with friends.

# ELEMENTO

15 Hatzorfim St.
Tel. (03) 620 9848
www.elemento-design.com
*Map/Carte* **7**

Established in 1998 by Yossy Goldberg, one of Israel's foremost designers, Elemento has for years been livening up homes, offices, hotels and other spaces locally and abroad with its unique line of furniture. Elemento's showroom in Israel is located in a stunning, enormous space set in a 500-year-old Ottoman-era building in Old Jaffa, where Goldberg's creations are on display in all their glorious color. Walking through the showroom, with its exposed brick and arched entryways, is in itself a remarkable experience, but the visit is made all the more enjoyable by the playfulness and bold patterns of Goldberg's designs. All of the piece—ranging from sofas and armchairs to work desks and dining tables—are manufactured locally in Israel and feature Goldberg's signature touch: pairing contemporary materials with design inspired by the 1960s and '70s. The showroom is a maze divided into several rooms, each with its exclusive color combination and atmosphere, that are united by the core DNA of Elemento's clear style. It also contains an area dedicated to wallpapers and fabrics, imported exclusively from high-end European designers. If you are looking to inject a dose of style and color into your life, Goldberg and his professional team of designers will gladly help—and make the process fun along the way.

## AISHA GALLERY
12 Yefet St.
(corner of Hahalfanim Alley)
Tel. (072) 273 2530
www.aisha.co.il
*Map/Carte 8*

Located in an ancient building in an enchanting alley reminiscent of those in Morocco, Aisha specializes in unique handcrafted pieces. From clothing to tableware, linen and textiles, furniture, cosmetics and more—all of Aisha's wares are made by local artists and craftsmen from the North African country. The gallery's pieces, culled from proprietor Aisha's frequent travels to Morocco, are individually handmade using classic techniques, and incorporate touches of contemporary design. Among the wares Aisha carries are hand-embroidered textiles, puff cushions and pillows, light fixtures, a line of handbags crafted using a traditional technique, mosaic marble tables, Egyptian cotton linens and rare collectors' items. Aisha offers a warm, authentic shopping experience, and also provides information about the artisans and their work methods in on-site lectures for design professionals and the general public.

### YOEZER WINE BAR
2 Yoezer Ish Habira St. • Tel. (03) 683 9115

Located in a picturesque Jaffa alley, Yoezer is a romantic, dimly lit wine bar set under the arches of a striking Ottoman-era stone structure. The menu features some of the city's finest French cuisine, along with an exceptional wine list that includes the widest selection of international vintages available in Israel.

### SOFI DESIGN
3 Rabbi Nachman St. • Tel. (03) 516 2077

This inviting design shop stocks an array of housewares, from silverware and teapots to wall calendars and clocks, along with textiles and baby accessories—all in a vibrant rainbow of colors. You'll be hard-pressed to leave here empty-handed and without a smile on your face.

### UMA GALLERY
5 Ben Yair St. • Tel. (03) 682 2290

If you're in search of African and tribal decorative objects, you'll find a nice selection at this spacious gallery.

### ILANA GOOR MUSEUM
4 Mazal Dagim St. • Tel. (03) 683 7676

Located in an impressive 18th-century building in the heart of Old Jaffa's gallery area, the Ilana Goor Museum showcases her distinctive sculptures and furniture, along with her art collection, culled from around the world.

### NA LAGA'AT CENTER
Jaffa Port • Tel. (03) 633 0808

Meaning "do touch" in Hebrew, Na Laga'at is a truly unique theater featuring a troupe of deaf-blind actors who perform original plays based on their own life experiences.

### SALOONA
17 Tirza St. • Tel. (03) 518 1719

Located in the artsy Noga Quarter, Saloona is one of the most stylish lounge bars in the city. It often hosts top-notch DJs and live music performances, as well as changing art exhibitions.

### PUAA
8 Rabbi Yochanan St. • Tel. (03) 682 3821

Puaa is located smack in the middle of the flea market, which is the source for its funky, vintage décor. This charming café is one of the most popular in Jaffa, and serves up vegetarian-friendly home-style and Mediterranean food, fresh salads and yummy desserts.

### CHARCUTERIE
3 Rabbi Hanina St. • Tel. (03) 682 8843

Set in the bustling flea market area, Charcuterie is the creation of Chef Vince Muster, whose extensive menu ranges from meats to pastas—all of which can be enjoyed in the pleasant alfresco dining area.

### CONTAINER
Jaffa Port • Tel. (03) 683 6321

Easily one of the most popular restaurant-bar spaces in Jaffa, the Container is set in a 1920s hangar facing the water and contains a 45-seat horseshoe-shaped bar. It attracts a chic clientele that flocks here for the chilled cocktails, fresh seafood and artistic vibe.

# GUSTA
16 Amiad St.
Tel. (03) 682 9752
19 Jabotinsky St.
Tel. (077) 323 0038
www.www.gusta.co.il
*Map/Carte 9*

Six years ago, Ayala Meromi-Keinan had an epiphany: Realizing that she wanted to work in fashion, she launched her clothing line, Gusta, with little formal training but much creativity and, well, gusto. The functional-yet-chic collection got its start at the designers' market in Dizengoff Center, and has grown into a successful brand with two stylish boutiques in equally fashionable locations—a recently opened branch near the Jaffa flea market, and another just off Dizengoff Street. Meromi-Keinan uses a broad range of fabrics, and her designs feature clean lines and a monochromatic palette, but always have an edge. Gusta is designed for modern women who want high-quality, comfortable clothes that make them look sophisticated yet at ease around the clock.

# MARGOZA
24 Margoza St.
Tel. (03) 681 7787
*Map/Carte* 10

Margoza lies at the heart of renewed Jaffa and is set against the colorful backdrop of the flea market. The French-style, family-run bakery opened its doors, ironically enough, two weeks before Passover in 2009, when the smell of its breads and pastries first wafted through the air. Since then, the aroma of its sweet and savory baked goods—all of which are handmade each morning on the premises—has turned Margoza into a local favorite, a place where you feel like part of the family. The bright, cozy space features a charming outdoor seating area, where you can enjoy a flaky pastry or sandwich, along with a perfectly prepared coffee that comes sealed with a meringue kiss.

---

*Restaurant • Restaurant*

## THE ITALIAN
16 Olei Zion St. • Tel. (03) 682 9678

This homey restaurant is set in an old Bauhaus building in the heart of the flea market. It features an open kitchen, where simple yet flavorful Italian fare is cooked up right before diners' eyes.

*Restaurant • Restaurant*

## SHAKUF
2 Magen Avraham St. • Tel. (03) 758 6888

Seating only 40 guests, Shakuf is designed as a sprawling open kitchen and provides a fresh interpretation of local ingredients and cuisine. The kitchen is run by Chef Eldad Shem-Tov, a rising star who has been schooled by both Alain Ducasse and Wylie Dufresne.

*Design • Design*

## KLEIN'S
11 Marzuk ve Azar St. • Tel. (03) 540 8565

This 1,100-square-meter design house provides high-end kitchens and baths to the super-posh upper echelons of Israeli society. Even people who can't afford it come here for inspiration.

---

*Fashion • Mode*

## SHARON BRUNSHER
13 Amiad St. • Tel. (03) 683 1896

Sharon Brunsher is renowned for her minimalist fashions that combine the finest materials with groundbreaking lines in a subdued, monochromatic palette. Her boutiques are more like lifestyle concept shops that carry apparel, bedding, textiles, accessories, paper products and fragrances, all designed and manufactured in Israel.

*Restaurant • Restaurant*

## HAZAKEN VE HAYAM
83 Kedem St. • Tel. (03) 681 8699

Meaning "the old man and the sea," this old-time seafood restaurant overlooking the Mediterranean serves the freshest catch accompanied by an abundance of salads at incredibly reasonable prices.

*Design • Design*

## GAPOROU GALLERY
6 Nachman St. • Tel. (03) 973 1007

Another gallery in the heart of the flea market, Gaporou imports tribal art from Africa, and specializes in textiles and other works combining tribal design with contemporary touches.

---

*Night • Nuit*

## SHAFFA BAR
2 Nachman St. • Tel. (03) 681 1205

Owned by the proprietors of the nearby hair salon of the same name, Shaffa is a funky bar in the flea market area that has become a neighborhood favorite thanks to its laid-back atmosphere and tasty upscale bar food. Shaffa occasionally throws fun street parties on Friday afternoons that are a perfect way to kick off the weekend.

*Restaurant • Restaurant*

## ALI KARAVAN
1 Hadolphin St.

Popularly called "Abu Hassan" after the late owner, this is widely considered the best hummus in Israel. Get there early—they close shop once the daily batch is gone.

*Fashion • Mode*

## UNA UNA
8 Rabbi Yochanan St. • Tel. (03) 518 4782

Almog Weiss and Mira Gafni are the designers behind this popular handcrafted shoe line that's a perfect fit for artistically inclined women of all ages.

# HERBERT

**10 Apak St.**
Tel. **(077) 550 1453**
www.**herbert**.co.il
*Map/Carte* **11**

Herzliya-born designer Omri Paecht is the visionary behind Herbert, a specialty furniture boutique whose pieces blur the line between indoor and outdoor design aesthetics. Herbert takes its name from Paecht's grandfather, who had a special affinity for carpentry and woodworking that was clearly imparted to his grandson. The bright, spacious showroom displays the younger Paecht's designs—including benches, consoles and tables of various sizes—which are skillfully crafted from richly textured, exotic types of wood, along with metals and other eco-friendly materials. The boutique also showcases outdoor furniture and fireplaces that are imported exclusively from firms FueraDentro in the Netherlands and Conmoto in Germany, and that complement Herbert's modern and green design philosophy. Herbert is appropriately located in the slightly industrial Noga Quarter, on the border between Tel Aviv and Jaffa, where artists, carpenters and silversmiths can often be seen mid-creation inside their studios.

# POYKE

14 Tirza St.
Tel. (03) 681 4622
www.poyke.com
*Map/Carte 12*

Located among the Noga Quarter's scenic cobblestone streets, Poyke was opened seven years ago by Chef Ariel Cohen, and takes it names from a type of pot that has been used for centuries in South Africa. The restaurant is a reflection of Chef Cohen's desire to offer patrons a comprehensive experience that includes African food, music and culture. The menu comprises hearty dishes from the South African kitchen, such as a slow-cooked beef stew with red wine, smoked entrecôte, biltong shrimp and a traditional maize porridge called mieliepap. Poyke also has an extensive wine list that features the best South African vintages. Make sure to save room for dessert—especially the decadent chocolate soufflé, which is baked in a poyke and oozes bubbling white chocolate.

# CHÂTELAINE

8 Raziel St.
Tel. (03) 683 3330
*Map/Carte 13*

Châtelaine is the result of a partnership between an interior designer and a jewelry designer, who infuse their unique gallery with creativity and passion. Located a short walk from Clock Tower Square and the flea market in Jaffa, this special gallery welcomes visitors with the subtle aroma of its international collection of luxury soaps, and introduces them to a world of classic and modern designs that make a statement. Châtelaine's one-of-a-kind pieces include armchairs and other furniture upholstered with vintage needlepoint pieces and additional embroidery; handcrafted contemporary jewelry; and works by up-and-coming Israeli artists. Each piece in the gallery is carefully selected by the proprietors, who are happy to share their exceptional creativity and passion.

*Restaurant • Restaurant*

### HOUSE NO. 3
3 Amiad St. • Tel. (03) 681 4052

Located opposite the flea market in a lovingly restored and beautifully decorated Ottoman-era building dating back to 1870, House No. 3 offers guests a special dining experience.

*Art • Art*

### URBAN GALLERY
12 Beit Eshel St. • Tel. (03) 518 1401

Urban Gallery specializes in the works of Israeli and international modern artists, and features changing exhibitions of works in different media. It also offers the largest selection of art by the renowned Menashe Kadishman.

*Night • Nuit*

### MARGOZA BAR
3 Rabbi Yochanan St. • Tel. (077) 450 1766

Margoza is a lively neighborhood bar centrally located in the flea market area. It's a great place to relax with a beer or glass of wine while getting in some quality people watching.

*Design • Design*

### WORKSHOP
15 Yefet St. • Tel. (03) 518 5928

Zvi and Hadas Shaham, a father-and-daughter design team, create an eclectic mix of furniture—including modern and restored retro pieces—along with accessories and jewelry.

*Night • Nuit*

### CHARCUTERIE – THE BAR
3 Rabbi Hanina St. • Tel. (03) 682 8843

At the bar adjacent to Charcuterie, Chef Vince Muster offers a lighter menu: cheese, sausages, smoked fish and other delicacies can be enjoyed with a glass of wine or cocktail. Early birds can treat themselves to breakfast.

*Design • Design*

### EXTRA VERGINE
1 Hapninim St. • Tel. (03) 682 2905

Nestled in an ancient Jaffa alley, this design studio and atelier carries beautiful lampshades and other decorative home accessories, all infused by what the proprietors call "Mediterranean attitude."

*Design • Design*

### 4 MAKE
32 Yefet St. • Tel. (03) 518 3212

Two industrial designers who studied together in Jerusalem own this showroom for unique decorative items, including colorful wall decals, clocks and artworks.

*Fashion • Mode*

### ALONA BAR YONA
10 Margoza St. • Tel. (03) 681 7875

Alona Bar Yona designs chic women's fashion, with clean lines and form-flattering shapes. She rounds out her collection with accessories from some of the best local designers.

*Concept Store • Magasin spécialisé*

### GRAPE MAN
12 Ba'al Haturim St. • Tel. (03) 518 0533

The Grape Man is the brainchild of wine enthusiast Haim Gan, considered one of the foremost authorities on wine in the country, whose goal is to nurture the growing wine culture in Israel. Located in a centuries-old building rumored to have been the first captured by Napoleon in 1799, the Grape Man contains a large wine bar/lounge, special areas for tastings and courses, along with a well-stocked wine shop.

## MUSEUMS

**Ben-Gurion House**
17 Ben-Gurion Blvd.
Tel. (03) 522 1010

**Bialik House**
22 Bialik St.
Tel. (03) 525 4530

**Bible House**
16 Rothschild Blvd.
Tel. (03) 517 7760

**Center for Contemporary Art**
5 Kalisher St.
Tel. (03) 510 6111
www.cca.org.il

**Beit Hatfutsot
(Diaspora Museum)**
Tel Aviv University Campus
Tel. (03) 745 7808
www.bh.org.il

**Eretz Israel Museum**
2 Haim Levanon St.
Tel. (03) 641 5244
www.eretzmuseum.org.il

**Genia Schreiber Gallery**
Gate 7, Tel Aviv University,
Ramat Aviv
Tel. (03) 640 8860

**Hagana Museum**
23 Rothschild Blvd.
Tel. (03) 560 8624

**HaPalmach Museum**
10 Haim Levanon St.
Tel. (03) 643 6393

**Helena Rubinstein Pavilion**
6 Tarsat Blvd.
Tel. (03) 528 7196
www.tamuseum.com

**Ilana Goor Museum**
4 Mazal Dagim St.
Tel. (03) 683 7676
www.ilanagoor.com

**Independence Hall**
16 Rothschild Blvd.
Tel. (03) 510 6426

**Israel Army Museum**
Yehezkel Koifman St.,
corner of Hamered St.
Tel. (03) 516 1346

**Jabotinsky Institute**
38 King George St.
Tel. (03) 528 7320
www.jabotinsky.org

**Nachum Gutman Museum**
21 Rokach St.
Tel. (03) 516 1970
www.gutmanmuseum.co.il

**Rokach House**
36 Rokach St.
Tel. (03) 516 8042
www.rokach-house.co.il

**Rubin Museum**
14 Bialik St.
Tel. (03) 525 5961
www.rubinmuseum.org.il

**Tel Aviv Museum of Art**
27 Shaul Hamelech Blvd.
Tel. (03) 607 7020
www.tamuseum.com

**Zaritsky Artists' House**
9 Alharizi St.
Tel. (03) 524 6685
www.artisthouse.co.il

## GALLERIES

**Alfred Gallery**
19 Levontin St.
Tel. (054) 541 2213

**Alon Segev Gallery**
6 Rothschild Blvd.
Tel. (03) 609 0769
www.alonsegevgallery.com

**Bineth Gallery**
15 Frishman St.
Tel. (03) 523 8910
www.binethgallery.com

**Braverman Gallery**
12B Hasharon St.
Tel. (03) 566 6162
www.bravermangallery.com

**Chelouche Gallery**
7 Mazeh St.
Tel. (03) 528 9713
www.chelouchegallery.com

**D&A Gallery**
57 Yehuda Halevi St.
Tel. (077) 450 8010
www.gallerydanda.co.il

**Dan Gallery**
36 Gordon St.
Tel. (03) 524 3968
www.finegallery.co.il

**DAP Dollinger Art Project**
18 Frishman St.
Tel. (03) 527 6994
www.dollingerartproject.com

**Dvir Gallery**
11 Nahum St.
11 Nitzana St.
Hangar 2, Jaffa Port
Tel. (03) 604 3003
www.dvirgallery.com

**Ehrlich Contemporary Art**
7 Yedidya Frenkel St.
Tel. (03) 681 9594
www.ehrlichgallery.com

**Farkash Gallery**
5 Mazal Dagim St.
Tel. (03) 683 4741
www.farkash-gallery.com

**Florentin 45**
45 Florentin St.
Tel. (03) 276 3249
www.florentin45.com

**Gallery 39**
9 Nachmani St.
Tel. (03) 566 6631
www.artgallery39.com

**Gallery Harel**
8 Elizabeth Bergner St.
Tel. (03) 681 6834
www.harelart.com

**Gal-On Gallery**
79-81 Yehuda Halevi St.
Tel. (03) 560 3222

**Gerstein Gallery**
99 Ben Yehuda St.
Tel. (03) 529 3826

**Givon Art Gallery**
35 Gordon St.
Tel. (03) 522 5427
www.givonartgallery.com

**Gordon Gallery**
95 Ben Yehuda St.
Tel. (03) 524 0323
www.gordongallery.co.il

**Hakibbutz Gallery**
25 Dov Hoz St.
Tel. (03) 523 2533
www.kibbutzgallery.org.il

**Hamidrasha Art Gallery**
34 Dizengoff St.
Tel. (03) 620 3129

**The Hayek Center**
4 Louis Pasteur St.
Tel. (03) 681 6446
www.hayekart.com

**TEL AVIV
CULTURE**

**Heder Art Gallery**
11 Gottlieb St.
Tel. (03) 522 2402
www.theheder.com

**Indie Gallery**
57 Yehuda Halevi St.
Tel. (077) 450 8010
www.galleryindie.com

**Inga**
7 Bar Yochai St.
Tel. (03) 518 1812
www.inga-gallery.com

**Julie M.**
10 Bezalel Yaffe St.
Tel. (03) 560 7005
www.juliem.com

**Kav 16**
6 Sheshet Hayamim St.,
Ramat Aviv, Neve Eliezer
Community Center
Tel. (03) 730 0360

**Litvak Gallery**
4 Berkovich St.
Tel. (03) 695 9496
www.litvakgallery.co.il

**Mika Gallery**
97 Ben Yehuda St.
Tel. (03) 952 5830
www.mikagallery.co.il

**Nelly Aman**
26 Gordon St.
Tel. (03) 523 2003
www.amangallery.co.il

**Noga Gallery**
60 Ahad Ha'am St.
Tel. (03) 566 0123
www.nogagallery.co.il

**P8 Gallery**
8 Poriah St.
Tel. (050) 861 6001

**Paradigma Design Gallery**
60 Ahad Ha'am St.
Tel. (03) 566 0333
www.paradigmagallery.com

**Peer**
42 Mazeh St.
Tel. (03) 528 2299

**Raw Art**
3 Shvil Hameretz St., Bldg. 8
Tel. (03) 683 2559
www.rawart-gallery.com

**Rosenfeld**
1 Shvil Hamifal St.
Tel. (03) 522 9044
www.rg.co.il

**Rothschild 69 Project**
12 Rothschild Blvd.
www.rothschild69.co.il

**Shay Arye Gallery**
61 Shlomo Hamelech St.
Tel. (03) 696 7196
www.shayaryegallery.com

**Solo Gallery**
7 Solomon St.
Tel. (03) 636 5720

**Sommer Contemporary Art**
13 Rothschild Blvd.
Tel. (03) 516 6400
www.sommergallery.com

**Stern**
30 Gordon St.
Tel. (03) 524 6303
www.sternart.com

**Tavi Dresdner**
24 Achva St.
Tel. (077) 787 0605
www.tavidresdner.com

**Tel Aviv Artists' Studio**
18 Elifelet St.
Tel. (03) 683 0505

**Yair Gallery**
6 Ibn Gvirol St.
Tel. (03) 695 6927
www.yairgallery.net

## CULTURAL CENTERS

**Beit Lessin Theater**
101 Dizengoff St.
Tel. (03) 725 5333
www.lessin.co.il

**Beit Ariela Cultural Center**
25 Shaul Hamelech Blvd.
Tel. (03) 691 0141

**Cameri Theatre**
30 Leonardo da Vinci St.
Tel. (03) 606 0960
www.cameri.co.il

**Habima – National Theater**
2 Tarsat Blvd.
Tel. (03) 526 6666
www.habima.org.il

**Gesher Theater**
9 Jerusalem Blvd.
Tel. (03) 681 3131

**Hasimta Theater**
8 Mazal Dagim St.
Tel. (03) 681 2126

**Institut Français de Tel-Aviv**
7 Rothschild Blvd.
Tel. (03) 796 80 00

**Israel Philharmonic Orchestra**
Mann Auditorium
1 Huberman St.
Tel. (03) 629 0193
www.ipo.co.il

**The Israeli Opera, Tel Aviv
Performing Arts Center**
19 Shaul Hamelech Blvd.
Tel. (03) 692 7700
www.israel-opera.co.il

**Mann Auditorium**
1 Huberman St.
Tel. (1700) 703 030
www.hatarbut.co.il

**Mayumana House**
15 Louis Pasteur St.
Tel. (03) 681 3131
www.mayumana.com

**Suzanne Dellal Center**
5 Yehieli St.
Tel. (03) 510 5656
www.suzannedellal.org.il

**Tmuna Theatre**
8 Soncino St.
Tel. (03) 562 9462
www.tmu-na.org.il

**Tzavta**
30 Ibn Gvirol St.
Tel. (03) 695 0156

**Zionist Organization
of America House**
26 Ibn Gvirol St.
Tel. (03) 695 9341

## MUSIC VENUES

**Barby**
52 Kibbutz Galuyot St.
Tel. (03) 518 8123
www.barby.co.il

**Felicja Blumental Music Center**
26 Bialik St.
Tel. (03) 6201185
www.fbmc.co.il

**Levontin 7**
7 Levontin St.
Tel. (03) 560 5084
www.levontin7.com

**Rothschild 12**
12 Rothschild Blvd.
Tel. (03) 510 6430
www.rothschild12.com

**Shablul Jazz Club**
Hangar 13, Tel Aviv Port
Tel. (03) 546 1891
www.shabluljazz.com

**Zappa**
24 Raoul Wallenberg St.,
Ramat Hachayal
Tel. (03) 767 4646
www.zappa-club.co.il

**Ozen Bar**
48 King George St.
Tel. (03) 03 621 5210
www.third-ear.com/ozenbar

## MOVIE THEATERS

**Tel Aviv Cinematheque**
2 Sprinzak St.
Tel. (03) 606 0800

**Dizengoff Cinema**
Dizengoff Center
Tel. (03) 620 3303

**Gat**
2 Zeitlin St.
Tel. (03) 696 7888

**Lev Dizengoff**
Dizengoff Center
Tel. (03) 621 2222

**Rav Chen Dizengoff**
Dizengoff Square
Tel. (03) 528 2288

# USEFUL INFORMATION

**Police** 100

**Medical Emergency** 101

**Fire Department** 102

**Tel Aviv–Jaffa City Hall**
69 Ibn Gvirol St.
Tel. (1599) 588 888
www.tel-aviv.gov.il

**Tourist Information Centers**
www.visit-tlv.com
AppStore App: Visit-tlv

46 Herbert Samuel St.
Tel. (03) 516 6188

Hatachana Complex,
Building No. 5
Tel. (03) 776 4005

**Post Offices**
170 Ibn Gvirol St.
Tel. (03) 604 1109

61 Hayarkon St.
Tel. (03) 510 0218

61 Herzl St.
Tel. (03) 682 5856
www.israelpost.co.il

**Hospital**
The Tel Aviv Sourasky Medical
Center (Ichilov Hospital)
6 Weizmann St.
Tel. (03) 697 4444

**Pharmacies**
London Ministore SuperPharm
4 Shaul Hamelech Blvd.
Tel. (03) 6960115

Allenby Street SuperPharm
115 Allenby St.
Tel. 510 4111

Gordon Street SuperPharm
129 Dizengoff St, corner of
Gordon St.
Tel. (03) 529 9566

**Taxis**
Balfour Taxis
59 Balfour St.
Tel. (03) 560 4545

Shekem Taxis
69 Gordon St.
Tel. (03) 527 0404

Habima Taxis
4 Tarsat Blvd.
Tel. (03) 528 3131

Hayarkon Taxis
101 Hayarkon St.
Tel. (03) 522 3233

Hatzafon Taxis
20 Yirmiyahu St.
Tel. (03) 602 0210

Nordau Taxis
16 Nordau St.
Tel. (03) 546 6222

**Road Service**
Shagrir
Tel. (03) 557 8888
www.shagrir.co.il

Europe Assistance
Tel. (03) 953 5600

**Transportation**
Egged Bus Company
Tel. (03) 694 8888
www.egged.co.il

Dan Bus Company
Tel. (03) 639 4444
www.dan.co.il

Israel Airports Authority
Ben-Gurion Airport
Tel. (03) 975 5555

Arrivals & Departures
Tel. (03) 972 3333
www.iaa.gov.il

Israel Railways
Tel. (03) 611 7000
www.israrail.org.il

**Credit Cards**
American Express
Tel. (03) 636 4292

MasterCard
Tel. (03) 636 4400

Visa
Tel. (03) 572 6666

# FREE WALKING TOURS

## Bauhaus - The White City
Every Saturday at 11:00
Meeting point: 46 Rothschild Boulevard
(corner of Shadal Street).

In July 2003, UNESCO proclaimed the "White City," the unique urban and historical fabric of Tel Aviv, a World Cultural Heritage site. The tour focuses on the architectural styles of the 1930s—most notably the International, or Bauhaus, style—along Rothschild Boulevard. Telling the story of Tel Aviv from its early years till today, this tour presents a wonderful opportunity to savor the experience of life, past and present, in the first Hebrew city.

## Tel Aviv by Night
Every Tuesday at 20:00
Meeting point: Corner of Rothschild Boulevard and Herzl Street (on the boulevard).

A night walking tour of Tel Aviv, depicting the foundation of the city through intriguing stories. The tour passes through Rothschild Boulevard, Nahalat Binyamin and the heart of Tel Aviv, and sheds light on the nighttime atmosphere that characterizes the local restaurants, bars and coffee shops in this area.

## Tel Aviv University: Art & Architecture
Every Monday at 11:00
*Except for Jewish holidays, the week of Sukkot, the week of Passover and during the last week of August.
Meeting point: Dyonon bookstore, university campus entrance (intersection of Haim Levanon and Einstein Streets).

An introduction to the Israeli architecture on campus, this tour delves into styles, international influences, stories of buildings and architects, environmental sculpture and landscape design. The tour is offered in cooperation with the Friends of Tel Aviv University.

## Old Jaffa
Every Wednesday at 9:30
Meeting point: Clock Tower (beginning of Yefet Street), Jaffa.

The tour embraces the picturesque flea market, archaeological sites, the view of Tel Aviv from the Crest Garden (Gan Hapisga) and the renovated alleys and buildings of historic Old Jaffa.

## GAY
## TEL AVIV

In recent years, Tel Aviv has transformed itself not only into one of the most cosmopolitan cities in the Middle East, but also into what *The New York Times* has dubbed the "new gay mecca of the Mediterranean." Tel Aviv is one of the most open, welcoming and tolerant cities around, which makes it a prime travel destination for the LGBT community. The city has a vibrant gay and lesbian scene, including a popular Pride Parade, film festivals, party nights and other cultural offerings. Most bars and clubs are gay-friendly, and many of them host weekly gay and lesbian party nights. For the most up-to-date listings, please visit the following websites:

**www.telavivgayvibe.com**

**www.gaywaytlv.com**

**www.gogay.co.il**

**www.gaycenter.org.il**

**www.atraf.com**

**Gay city tour**
Every Friday at 10 am: telling the story of Tel Aviv and the gay community.
Book online at: www.telavivgayvibe.com

**Gay Community Center**
Meir Garden; Open daily 9:00-21:00

**Tel Aviv Gay Pride Parade**
Will take place on:

10.06.2011

08.06.2012

07.06.2013

## RESTAURANTS

**Nanuchka** 145
30 Lilienblum St.
Tel. (03) 516 2254

**NG** 134
6 Ahad Ha'am St.
Tel. (03) 516 7888

**Noa Bistro** 171
14 Hatzorfim St.
Tel. (03) 518 4668

**Onami** 76
18 Ha'arba'a St.
Tel. (03) 562 1172

**Orna & Ella** 42
33 Sheinkin St.
Tel. (03) 620 4753

**Pasta Mia** 42
10 Wilson St.
Tel. (03) 561 0189

**Place for Meat** 139
64 Shabazi St.
Tel. (03) 510 4020

**Poyke** 180
14 Tirza St.
Tel. (03) 681 4622

**Pronto** 134
4 Herzl St.
Tel. (03) 566 0915

**Radio Rosco** 50
97 Allenby St.
Tel. (03) 560 0334

**Rak Basar** 116
14 Raoul Wallenberg St.
Tel. (03) 644 4822

**Raphael** 80
87 Hayarkon St.
Tel. (03) 522 6464

**Rokach 73** 116
73 Rokach St.
Tel. (03) 744 8844

**Ronimotti** 112
24 Raoul Wallenberg St.
Tel. (03) 647 0247

**Rothschild's Kitchen** 44
73 Rothschild Blvd.
Tel. (03) 525 7171

**Ruben** 116
32 Yirmiyahu St.

**Seatara** 112
Sea & Sun
Tel. (03) 699 6633

**Segev Express** 109
38 Habarzel St.
Tel. (03) 944 3115

**Shakuf** 178
2 Magen Avraham St.
Tel. (03) 758 6888

**Shila** 104
128 Ben Yehuda St.
Tel. (03) 522 1224

**Social Club** 49
45 Rothschild Blvd.
Tel. (03) 560 1114

**Stefan Braun** 45
99 Allenby St.
Tel. (03) 560 4725

**Sushi Samba TLV** 116
27 Habarzel St.
Tel. (03) 644 4345

**Suzanna** 140
9 Shabazi St.
Tel. (03) 5177580

**Tapas Ahad Ha'am** 50
27 Ahad Ha'am St.
Tel. (03) 566 6966

**Tapeo** 76
16 Ha'arba'a St.
Tel. (03) 624 0484

**Thai House** 76
8 Bograshov St.
Tel. (03) 517 8568

**Tony Vespa** 110
280 Dizengoff St.
Tel. (03) 546 0000

**Toto** 72
4 Berkovich St.
Tel. (03) 693 5151

**Turkiz** 110
Sea & Sun Beach
Tel. (03) 699 6306

**Vicky Cristina** 142
Hatachana
Tel.(03) 736 7272

**Yakimono** 50
19 Rothschild Blvd.
Tel. (03) 517 5173

**Yavne Montefiore** 49
31 Montefiore St.
Tel. (03) 566 6189

**Yoezer Wine Bar** 176
2 Yoezer Ish Habira St.
Tel. (03) 683 9115

**Yulia** 112
Tel Aviv Port
Tel. (03) 546 9777

**Zepra** 82
96 Yigal Alon St.
Tel. (03) 624 0044

## CAFÉ

**Anita Ice Cream** 136
42 Shabazi St.
Tel. (03) 517 0505

**Alkalay** 104
1 Alkalay St.
Tel. (03) 604 1260

**Amelia** 81
88 Dizengoff St.
Tel. (03) 528 3888

**Baccio** 86
85 King George St.
Tel. (03) 528 9753

**Bakery** 83
72 Ibn Gvirol St.
Tel. (03) 696 1050

**Bakery** 37
13 Yad Harutzim St.
Tel. (03) 537 1041

**Bakery 29** 52
29 Ahad Ha'am St.
Tel. (03) 560 2020

**Café 12** 53
12 Rothschild Blvd.
Tel. (03) 510 6430

**Café Michal** 118
230 Dizengoff St.
Tel. (03) 523 0236

**Café Noah** 42
91 Ahad Ha'am St.
Tel. (03) 629 3799

**Café Tachtit** 42
9 Lincoln St.
Tel. (03) 736 2643

**Café Tamar** 42
57 Sheinkin St.
Tel. (03) 685 2376

**Dallal – The Bakery** 132
7 Kol Israel Haverim St.

**Dinitz** 45
22 Nahalat Binyamin St.
Tel. (03) 510 4665

**Hemda** 116
109 Ibn Gvirol St.
Tel. (074) 702 4664

**Iceberg Volcano** 106
Tel Aviv Port
Tel. (03) 602 6000

**Idelson 10** 106
252 Ben Yehuda St.
Tel. (03) 544 4154

**Jeremiah** 104
306 Dizengoff St.
Tel. (077) 793 1840

**La Gaterie** 110
184 Ben Yehuda St.
Tel. (077) 218 0077

**Lilush** 86
73 Frishman St.
Tel. (03) 537 9354

**Lulu Café Patisserie** 106
5 Alkalay St.
Tel. (057) 737 0443

**Margoza** 178
24 Margoza St.
Tel.(03) 681 7787

**Masaryk Cafe** 82
12 Masaryk Square
Tel. (03) 527 2411

**Mazzarine** 52
42 Montefiore St.
Tel. (03) 566 7020

**Movieing Cafe** 106
308 Dizengoff St.
Tel. (03) 544 4434

**Napoleon Patisserie** 172
15 Kedumim Square
Tel. (077) 403 0258

**Nechama Vahetzi** 45
144 Ahad Ha'am St.
Tel. (03) 685 2326

**Puaa** 176
8 Rabbi Yochanan St.
Tel. (03) 682 3821

**Reviva and Celia** 80
24 Ha'arba'a St.
Tel. (03) 561 8617

**Rothschild's** 52
Rothschild Blvd.,
Corner of Mazeh St.

**Savta Ice Cream** 136
9 Yehieli St.
Tel. (03) 510 5545

**Shine** 86
39 Shlomo Hamelech St.
Tel. (03) 527 6186

**Siach Café**  52
50 Sheinkin St.
Tel. (03) 528 6352

**Swing Café**  52
142 Rothschild Blvd.
Tel. (03) 560 0874

**Tazza D'oro**  139
6 Ahad Ha'am St.
Tel. (03) 516 6329

**The Streets**  86
2 Hanevi'im St.
Tel. (03) 620 1070

**Vaniglia**  109
22 Ashtori Haparchi St.
Tel. (03) 602 0185

**Zorik**  109
4 Yehuda Hamaccabi St.
Tel. (03) 604 8858

## NIGHT

**223**  104
223 Dizengoff St.

**Abraxas**  136
40 Lilienblum St.
Tel. (03) 510 4435

**Armadillo**  49
51 Ahad Ha'am St.
Tel. (03) 620 5573

**Armadillo Cerveza**  82
174 Dizengoff St.
Tel. (03) 529 3277

**Auto 76**  76
76 Ibn Gvirol St.

**Bar Barbunia**  104
192 Ben Yehuda St.
Tel. (03) 524 0961

**Bar Hanevi'im**  110
54 Yirmiyahu St.
Tel. (03) 605 6575

**Breakfast Club**  38
6 Rothschild Blvd.

**Bugsy**  151
28 Florentin St.
Tel. (03) 681 3138

**The Cat & the Dog**  72
23 Carlebach St.

**Charcuterie – The Bar**  181
3 Rabbi Hanina St.
Tel. (03) 682 8843

**Corduroy**  52
99 Allenby St.

**Dizengoff**  86
16 Ben Ami St.

**Eliezer**  112
186 Ben Yehuda St.
Tel. (03) 527 5961

**Galina**  106
Tel Aviv Port
Tel. (03) 544 5553

**Gazoz**  106
Hangar 1, Tel Aviv Port

**Gilda**  49
64 Ahad Ha'am St.
Tel. (03) 560 3588

**Hamara**  82
87 Hayarkon St.
Tel. (03) 522 6464

**Hamarkid**  50
30 Ibn Gvirol St.

**Haoman 17**  139
88 Abarbanel St.
Tel. (03) 681 3636

**Haprozdor**  50
1 Herzl St.

**Jaffa Bar**  172
30 Yefet St.
Tel. (03) 518 4668

**Jajo**  134
47 Shabazi St.
Tel. (03) 516 4557

**Jajo Vino**  136
44 Shabazi St.
Tel. (03) 510 0620

**Juno**  110
1 De Haas St.
Tel. (03) 544 6620

**Levontin 7**  50
7 Levontin St.
Tel. (03) 560 5084

**Lucifer**  50
97 Allenby St.
Tel. (03) 685 1666

**Margoza Bar**  181
3 Rabbi Yochanan St.
Tel. (077) 450 1766

**Mendalimos**  136
102 Hayarkon St.
Tel. (050) 846 4462

**Milk**  38
6 Rothschild Blvd.

**Molly Bloom's**  79
2 Mendele St.
Tel. (03) 522 1558

**Par Derrière**  38
4 King George St.
Tel. (03) 629 2111

**Peacock**  79
14 Marmorek St.
Tel. (03) 628 8259

**Radio E.P.G.B.**  45
7 Shadal St.
Tel. (03) 560 3636

**Rosa Parks**  109
256 Dizengoff St.
Tel. (03) 544 4881

**Rothschild 12**  53
12 Rothschild Blvd.
Tel. (03) 510 6430

**Saloona**  176
17 Tirza St.
Tel. (03) 518 1719

**Sex Boutique**  72
122 Dizengoff St.
Tel. (03) 544 4555

**Shaffa Bar**  178
2 Rabbi Nachman St.
Tel. (03) 681 1205

**Shampina**  42
32 Rothschild Blvd.
Tel. (03) 560 8852

**Shushka Shvili**  151
Hatachana
Tel. (03) 516 0008

**Shushu**  116
20 Yirmiyahu St.

**Silon**  82
129 Ibn Gvirol St.
Tel. (03) 546 4096

**Sublet**  139
6 Koifman St.
Tel. (054) 544 8444

**Taxidermy**  52
18 Harakevet St.

**Va'ad Habayit**  42
64 Rothschild Blvd.

**Wine Bar Boutique**  86
83 King George St.
Tel. (03) 525 9911

**Zinger**  49
49 Mazeh St.
Tel. (03) 686 8897

**Zizi Tripo**  49
7 Carlebach St.
Tel. (03) 561 1597

## HOTELS

**Artplus Hotel**  70
35 Ben Yehuda St.
Tel. (03) 797 1700

**Brown TLV Urban Hotel**  141
25 Kalisher St.
Tel. (03) 717 0200

**Center Chic Hotel**  70
2 Zamenhof St.
Tel. (03) 526 6100

**Cinema Hotel**  81
1 Zamenhof St.
Tel. (03) 520 7100

**Hotel Montefiore**  35
36 Montefiore St.
Tel. (03) 564 6100

**Leonardo Boutique**  112
17 Habarzel St.
Tel. (03) 511 0066

**Melody Hotel**  118
220 Hayarkon St.
Tel. (03) 521 5300

**Neve Tzedek Hotel**  138
4 Degania St.
Tel. (054) 207 0706

**Prima Tel Aviv**  84
105 Hayarkon St.
Tel. (03) 520 6666

**Sea Executive Suites**  45
76 Herbert Samuel St.
Tel. (03) 795 3434

**Shalom Hotel & Relax**  115
216 Hayarkon St.
Tel. (03) 524 3277

**The Varsano Hotel**  146
16 Hevrat Shas St.
Tel. (077) 554 5500

## FASHION

**A+**  72
172 Dizengoff St.
Tel. (03) 527 1728

**Alma**  45
9 Merkaz Ba'alei Melacha St.
Tel. (03) 620 0145

**Alona Bar Yona**  181
10 Margoza St.
Tel. (03) 681 7875

**Aluma**   110
9 Ashtori Haparchi St.
Tel. (03) 604 6095

**American Vintage**   151
Hatachana
Tel. (03) 510 4441

**Anat Mikulinsky**   79
121 Dizengoff St.
Tel. (03) 523 5180

**Anna K**   72
75 Frishman St.
Tel. (03) 529 1244

**Anya Fleet**   76
21 Masaryk Square
Tel. (03) 523 7497

**B Knit**   109
238 Dizengoff St.
Tel. (03) 544 4227

**Bait Banamal -
Comme il Faut**   119
Hangar 26, Tel Aviv Port
Tel. (03) 602 0521

**Babette**   136
31 Shabazi St.
Tel. (03) 510 0534

**Banker**   104
210 Dizengoff St.
Tel. (03) 529 0358

**Banot – Loulou Liam**   112
212 Dizengoff St.
Tel. (03) 529 1175

**Bellinky Oolalaa**   148
Hatachana
Tel. (03) 736 2828

**Butterfly**   151
Hatachana
Tel. (03) 516 3636

**Cala**   80
184 Dizengoff St.
Tel. (03) 529 0260

**Chucha**   48
43 Sheinkin St.
Tel. (03) 629 1841

**Daniella Lehavi**   36
21 Rothschild Blvd.
Tel. (03) 629 4044
34 Basel St.
Tel. (03) 544 0573

**Delicatessen**   49
4 Barzilay St.
Tel. (03) 560 2297

**Elise**   150
30 Shabazi St.
Tel. (03) 517 2835
25 Shabazi St.
Tel. (03) 510 9279

**Fablab Fabiani**   105
280 Dizengoff St.
Tel. 972 3 602 5569

**Frau Blau**   42
8 Hahashmal St.
Tel. (03) 560 1735

**Gertrud**   106
255 Dizengoff St.
Tel. (03) 546 7747

**Gusta**   177
16 Amiad St.
Tel. (03) 682 9752
19 Jabotinsky St.
Tel. (077) 323 0038

**Hanut Bgadim**   86
78 Dizengoff St.
Tel. (03) 529 3277

**Heartbreaker**   102
203 Dizengoff St.
Tel. (03) 522 0131

**Ido Recanati**   79
13 Malchei Israel St.
Tel. (03) 529 8481

**INN7**   108
177 Ben Yehuda St.
Tel. (03) 620 1022

**Imuma**   76
144 Dizengoff St.
Tel. (077) 443 0632

**Kay**   72
159 Dizengoff St.
Tel. (03) 522 9552

**Kisim**   50
8 Hahashmal St.
Tel. (03) 560 4890

**Leibling**   80
63 Bar Kochva St.
Tel. (03) 525 1020

**L'etranger**   134
3 Lilienblum St.
Tel. (03) 510 5171

**Lilamist**   109
280 Dizengoff St.
Tel. (03) 544 5048

**Maya Negri**   110
132 Jabotinsky St.
Tel. (03) 695 5133

**Mayu**   76
7 Malchei Israel St.
Tel. (03) 527 3992

**Mayu**   139
15 Shabazi St.
Tel. (03) 516 6975

**Mayu Outlet**   110
209 Dizengoff St.
Tel. (03) 522 2877

**Mor ve Yos**   38
13 Barzilay St.
Tel. (077) 322 3375

**Oberson Fashion House**   82
36 Gordon St.
Tel. (03) 524 3822

**Precious**   79
63 Frishman St.
Tel. (03) 529 3814

**Rhus Ovata**   72
159 Dizengoff St.
Tel. (03) 736 2643

**Ronen Chen**   80
155 Dizengoff St.
Tel. (03) 527 5672

**Roni Kantor**   52
64 Rothschild Blvd., 1st floor
Tel. (074) 703 3488

**Salon Salome**   82
25 Gordon St.
Tel. (03) 527 4150

**Sarah Braun**   79
162 Dizengoff St.
Tel. (03) 529 9902

**Shani Bar**   80
151 Dizengoff St.
Tel. (03) 527 8451

**Sharon Brunsher**   178
13 Amiad St.
Tel. (03) 683 1896

**Shine**   80
12 Masaryk Square
Tel. (03) 529 8607

**Skalski Leather Boutique**   139
19 Abulafia St.
Tel. (03) 683 4505

**Sketch**   134
Hatachana
Tel. (03) 962 8299

**Story**   43
60 Sheinkin St.
Tel. (03) 560 3911

**Story**   107
246 Dizengoff St.
Tel. (03) 544 8911

**Suzie Bergman**   109
21 Yirmiyahu St.
Tel. (077) 632 9031

**Take a Nap**   72
17 Masaryk Square
Tel. (03) 527 1757

**TES Leather Bags**   109
33 Basel St.
Tel. (03) 560 1482

**The Brunch**   76
17 Gordon St.
Tel. (03) 602 1602

**Theodora**   150
51 Geula St.
Tel. (052) 360 2690

**Umbrella**   116
252 Dizengoff St.
Tel. (03) 546 3867

**Una Una**   178
8 Rabbi Yochanan St.
Tel. (03) 518 4782

**Yanga**   86
69 Dizengoff St.
Tel. (03) 620 1115

**Yosef**   109
213 Dizengoff St.
Tel. (03) 529 8991

## DESIGN / ART

**4 Make**   181
32 Yefet St.
Tel. (03) 518 3212

**Aisha Gallery**   176
12 Yefet St.
Tel. (072) 273 2530

**Arbitman's**   77
31 Gordon St.
Tel. (03) 527 8254

**Armani Casa**   104
3 Hata'arucha St.
Tel. (03) 544 3306

**Arik Ben Simhon**   136
110 Nahalat Binyamin St.
Tel. (03) 683 7865

**Art Maroc**   151
38 Shabazi St.
Tel. (03) 516 1326